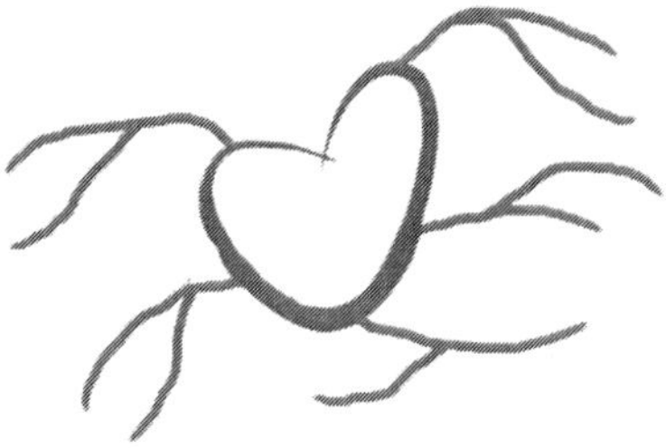

For you whose heart is filled with an abundance of things to say to the world.

THE HEART OF PUBLIC SPEAKING

CREATIVE STRATEGIES AND TECHNIQUES FOR EFFECTIVE PUBLIC SPEAKING

RAJU MANDHYAN

EMBASSY BOOKS
www.embassybooks.in

This edition first published in 2017

Published in India by:
Embassy Book Distributors
120, Great Western Building,
Maharashtra Chamber of Commerce Lane,
Fort, Mumbai - 400 023.
Tel : (91-22) 22819546 / 22818567.
Email : info@embassybooks.in
Website : www.embassybooks.in

Distribution Centres:
Mumbai, Ahmedabad, Bangalore, Kolkata, Chennai, Hyderabad,
New Delhi, Pune

ISBN: 978-93-86450-13-5

In my opinion . . .

Public Speaking is not just about standing up and speaking engagingly to a large number of people. It is about continuing the buildup of collective knowledge. It is about ripping open your psyche and finding out what makes you worth anything, and it is about tearing down beliefs and then building new ones.

Public Speaking is also about sharing and building knowledge. Knowledge that we own as a civilization and as individuals has been passed on from one generation to another more by speech than by any other form of communication. What we know and apply today is the accumulation of all thought from the dawn of civilization. And the depth and continuity of those thoughts is owed to the skill of Public Speaking.

The moment a person learns to express himself with clarity, creativity, and conscientiousness, he learns to grasp valuable insights about his desires and his deeds. The moment he understands himself, he begins to see the world in a better light and understanding. Soon, his behavior towards himself and the world becomes objective, fair, and empathic.

Several years ago, my eldest son took up debating in college and, at first, he just wanted to look good while he was speaking, then he wanted to become a good speaker, and today he is completely dedicated to becoming a speaker of good things.

These facets of Public Speaking put together become factors of change and renaissance. Over time saints, philosophers, and leaders mastered themselves by learning to communicate with authenticity and conviction. Their self-mastery and eloquence were fundamental in bringing about renaissance and positive change for humanity.

And so, it is with great humility that I invite you to rip open your psyche, find out what makes you worth anything, and become a creator of change by mastering the skill of Public Speaking.

Raju Mandhyan
Manila, Philippines 2016

I owe it all to . . .

A little over seven years ago, as the vice president of a business organization, I was to do the closing remarks for our national sales conference. Prior to this, all the training in public speaking I had received was just one lecture session in my business management class. I had made several sales, marketing, and basic business presentations during the course of work, and I considered myself to be substantially competent at public speaking.

On the evening before the event, I had a chat with the president of our division who was to do the opening remarks for the conference. I read him my script with the intention of avoiding redundancy in our talks. He was impressed with my choice of words and the way I had strung them together.

The next evening at the conference, in the presence of six regional heads and over a hundred sales managers, my immediate superior, the President of our division, delivered the opening remarks which contained nearly 70% of my scripted presentation! He had stolen my speech. I was flabbergasted!

For the next thirty minutes, my emotions shifted from shock, to anger, and then to rage. Should I expose him as a thief of thoughts or should I just say something totally new? In that state of confusion and anger I stepped up on the podium and froze. I did not know what to say or do. I couldn't complain or blame him because I had no proof! And even if I had, I would look really stupid lamenting over how my superior stole my words. When I finally raised my eyes and looked at the audience, my brain stopped and my mouth dried up. I just mumbled a few meaningless words and walked away from that meeting with my head hung low.

Back home, I couldn't stop thinking of what had happened. I should have had the alacrity, the presence of mind, and the wit to come up with something new – something interesting for the moment. Just because someone else had been a louse didn't mean that I had to be the patsy.

From that day on I decided that I would learn to speak off the cuff. I would learn to be confident, profound, and witty at the same time.

A few weeks later, I walked into the Executive Toastmasters Club of Makati, Philippines and delivered my Icebreaker. The late Mario Garrolinni, a Distinguished Toastmaster, was in the audience. After the meeting, he walked up to me and said, "You are good!" Mario was an Italian hippie who had lived the last twenty years of his life eating, drinking, and sleeping with all kinds of public speakers from different parts of the world. He was a public speaking junkie.

It was not so much the words he had uttered which complimented me, but more with what he did after saying, "You are good!" He looked at me in the face and smacked his lips. Nope, he didn't think I was delicious! But he did believe that my speaking style had the potential for delighting many an audience. I took that smacking of lips as a true, non-verbal compliment upon which I have built my destiny.

After Mario Garrolinni came hundreds and thousands of Toastmasters, trainers, and public speakers who gifted me with a little bit of themselves every time they spoke to me.

This book is the direct result of the sharing, the support, and at times a direct involvement of all those friends of mine, especially the following:

Padma Mangharam Siap, Trainer, Teacher of Arts, and a Giving Soul;

Jess Liwanag, News Reporter, Producer, Champion Speaker, and a Smiling Soul;

Adrian Martinez, Teacher, Trainer, and a Philosopher.

The depths, if any, in this book are the faults of these three.

And the most influential person in making this book easy, funny, and wholesome is my daughter Karishma. Every word, every idea, and every thought expressed in this book caused her eyes to light up and smile. These gestures of hers, to me, were as inspiring as Mario's lip smacking several years ago.

All of them sometimes watched me from a distance and then there were times when they gently grabbed me by the scruff of my neck and shoved me in the direction that I really wanted to go.

I do hope that this book does something similar for you. I hope it holds you by the elbow and guides you in the direction you want to go.

Raju Mandhyan
Manila, Philippines 2016

About this New Edition . . .

It has been three years since the release of the first edition of The Heart of Public Speaking. Trainers and those in the public speaking profession have expressed appreciation for the depths of the concepts, the simplicity of the examples and the usability of the techniques in the book. Others have loved the stories and the creative technique of Mind Mapping® for researching, structuring and internalizing ideas.

With this slightly updated version and enhanced layout I hope to reach a wider audience, especially those with an artistic tilt to their personalities and professions. This layout has been softened in appearance and allows the book to be more interactive and pleasant.

I hope you enjoy reading it as much as I have enjoyed enhancing it.

Raju Mandhyan
June 2016, Philippines

How to use this book . . .

This book is written and designed in such a way that you can approach public speaking not just as a skill, but more of a competency. It is written so that you will be able to do a lot of personal work internally and then create and deliver an effective, authentic talk externally.

Here are some guidelines for you to make the most out of this book:

- Read through the book several days before your speaking event. It will ease your thinking about the event and help you plan, write, and prepare calmly.
- The texts with a wide layout are things to do while the narrow layout contains discussions and concepts.
- Use the wide margins and available spaces to put in comments and reactions that way you will be interacting with me.
- Review the insights often after you have read the book. Apply all the techniques described frequently.
- Though the exercises may seem simple, please attempt to do them all. Make copies of them and review them as many times as you are called upon to speak.
- Take up Mind Mapping® and approach making presentations in a more flexible and a creative manner.

Please feel free to contact me for questions and further support.

Enjoy!

This book would not have come together without the help of:

Editors

- Katrina Letargo
- Asheesh Mandhyan

Guys, Thank you very much!

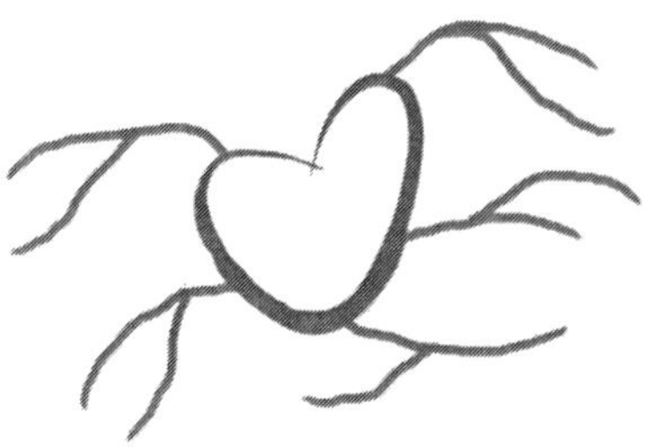

Get FREE INSIGHTS!

If you want to receive my sometimes deep and sometimes light-hearted articles on Communications, Creativity, and Leadership, please log on to www.mandhyan.com

what's inside for you . . .

Chapter One
Researching for a Speech

In the business world an executive knows something about everything, a technician knows everything about something, and the switchboard operator knows everything.

- Harold Coffin

The Multi-Sensory Approach to Learning

Before you go deeper into the nuances of public speaking, it would be beneficial to understand how a person absorbs, retains, processes, recalls, and reacts to external stimulus.

At any given moment, all our senses – the sense of sight, sound, smell, taste, and touch – are constantly working. When a person is seated in the audience, not only is he aware of the presence of the speaker and his surroundings, but he also receives, processes, and responds constantly to information picked up by his eyes, ears, taste buds, nostrils, and skin. The light in the room or outside the window, the sound of air conditioning, the taste of the last cup of coffee in his mouth, the scent of the person next to him, the texture of the chair he's sitting on – all these are constant providers of information to his brain.

As a speaker, you have to take all of these stimuli into account. You ought to be conscious and sensitive to the temperament, physiological needs, and comforts of your audience. You have to create, plan, and deliver a presentation with extreme sensitivity not just to the knowledge base and mindset of your audience, but also to their multi-sensorial nature.

The human mind is the sum of man's cognitive skills, perceptions, and intelligence, his state of mind, temperament, emotions, passions, and desires. Though man is complete by himself, he is still a part of his environment, community, and the universe.

Even though you have to address large crowds, you must realize that it is not possible to herd all your listeners together as one entity. Rather, you should see the group as a patchwork of several small parts held together by the essence of your message.

Understanding the Human Mind and Its Learning Styles

When it comes to learning, studies show that there are three types of people: the Visual, the Auditory, and the Kinesthetic learner.

Visual learners are people who like to see pictures in their minds. These people, when spoken to, convert words into mental pictures much faster than others. They are drawn to paintings, art, and images. When they speak, they describe things vividly, and when they listen, they literally see people's words forming images in their minds.

They like to actually see what you are talking about and seek out presentations supported by visual images, multimedia, flipcharts, and brochures.

Visual people make statements like:

- *"Do you see what I mean?"*
- *"I see where you are coming from."*
- *"Can you imagine the size of that cheesecake?"*

Visual learners make up about 35% of your audience. For these people, a speaker must fill his presentations with visuals and describe images vividly.

Auditory learners are people who can absorb, understand, and retain words, lists, and other information and recall them, more or less, in the original form. Auditory learners don't really need to see as many slides, brochures, or pictures as Visual learners. They can easily listen to lengthy presentations. They also like to speak at length themselves. These are people who can carry on a good conversation in person, in meetings, or on the telephone.

They often remember concepts and ideas in the exact words as described to them.

Auditory learners may make statements like:

- *"I hear you completely."*
- *"We have already talked about it."*
- *"Your explanation was clear as a bell to me."*

These people make up 25% of your audience, and for them, a speaker must fill his presentations with clear and precise words. Abstractions, analogies, and implied metaphors are not very effective for these kinds of people.

Kinesthetic learners are people who like to touch and feel things more than seeing pictures or listening to descriptions. In shops and stores, you see them picking up items, sniffing and weighing them. These are people who get physically close to you while conversing or talking. Kinesthetic learners are the huggers of the world. During public speaking events, they are the ones who like emotions and passions expressed in your spiels. They are the kind of people who generally look for the "human factor" in every interaction.

Kinesthetic people make statements like:

- *"That statement just doesn't feel right."*
- *"Let me get a grab on what you are trying to say."*
- *"My instinct tells me this will work!"*

These people make up 40% of your audience. A speaker or a presenter talking to them must bring real samples of products and fill his talk with stories of passion and examples so concrete that they can be touched.

Here are a few sample words from the three learning styles. Increased usage of words from any of the styles can make your talks either vivid, verbal or ones that generate feelings. In Chapter 3, I have also shown sample sentences for the Visual, Auditory and Kinesthetic audiences.

Visual Words	**Auditory Words**	**Kinesthetic Words**
Gigantic	Loud	Painful
Square	Shrieking	Harsh
Shapely	Mellow	Warm
Undulating	Sharp	Silky
Mountainous	Grating	Stony

How Memory Works: FORCE

Have you ever tried rearranging books on a shelf? When you place the first book on the shelf, there is a tendency to pause, look, and feel the book. You glance at the title and decide where it should go. That location becomes your primary reference point. From there, you pick up more books and arrange them either by how long you've had them, how often you refer to them, how relevant they are to your profession, how different they are from the other books, or if they are books that you are currently reading. More often than not, each group of books develops a certain "neighborhood" of their own.

Ponder how you do these things and you will recognize that your memory – which is an internal "bookshelf" – also works in a similar manner.

I like to refer to these mechanics of memory in an acronym: FORCE:

F for First:
In your memory, first impressions, words, and thoughts take primary importance. You have probably caught yourself talking

about the first time you met someone or the first time you ever rode a plane. Firsts are hard to forget.

The opening lines of a speech or the first questions you ask your audience are therefore very important. This is also referred to as the "Law of Primacy."

O for Often:

You easily remember things you often hear, see, or read. People you see regularly on the bus, a billboard on the way to work, or a song played again and again – these things you hear or feel can make a lasting impression in your memory. Though I am not a fond supporter of this repetition or rote in education, it works well in public speaking. Repeating certain lines or rephrasing lines while maintaining their meaning or essence reinforces the point better. This is also referred to as the "Law of Repetition."

R for Relate:

You easily recall things that appeal to you as a person. You can remember things such as a face in a crowd that may have features similar to your own or someone who is wearing a shirt in your favorite color.

You tend to remember ideas and beliefs that grow on the ones you already hold dear or things you have personally elaborated upon.

In public speaking, talking about ideas and subjects that the audience can associate with their knowledge and personalities builds better and quicker rapport. This is also called the "Law of Relevance."

C for Catchy:

It is hard to forget details or objects that are strikingly different from their environment, like a big white man in a crowd of Asians.

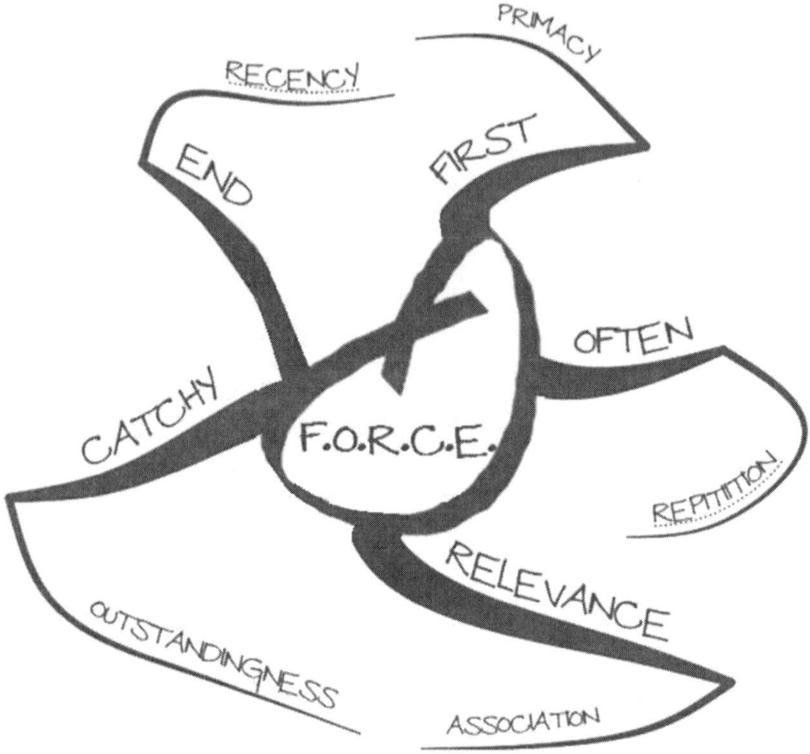

FORCE of Memory, or how the brain stores data forms the first layer to preparing for your speech. An awareness of this will help you construct speeches that can easily become memorable.

In public speaking, it is a good idea to create catchy hooks (like the acronym FORCE) and integrate them into the concepts and proposals of your presentations. This is also referred to as the "Law of Outstanding-ness."

E for End:

People tell dozens of stories about having seen someone for the very last time or their recent visit to a foreign land. In stories, books, and movies, authors like to create unforgettable endings to make a lasting impression. Things that are heard, seen, or felt at the end stay longer on the "desktop" of your memory.

They are always twice as fresh as the things filed in your mind for future reference. That is why in public speaking it is essential to pack your closings with a punch. This is also referred to as the "Law of Recency."

Speeches that are crafted according to the mechanics of FORCE are easy to absorb, understand, and recall. When we research materials to include in our presentations, we need to develop a keen eye for ideas and facts that:

- will create a good First impression;
- can be mentioned Often but in different words;
- the audience can Relate to easily;
- are different and Catchy;
- will create a lasting impression in the End.

As you work towards preparing and writing your speech, make a gentle effort to sprinkle all information with emotions. Research has it that when you attach feelings to information the memory lasts longer. The factors of FORCE combined with emotions form one of the layers of the Heart of Public Speaking.

Mind Mapping®: Rationale, Benefits & Applications

Mind Mapping® is a fun and simple technique that can help you analyze more efficiently and boost your creativity in expressing ideas. Originated by creativity expert Tony Buzan, Mind Mapping® has done wonders for my learning, thinking, and speaking skills.

I came upon this technique several years ago while I was conducting a presentation skills workshop for the British Council in Manila. A young Englishwoman with bright eyes and an easy smile sat through my workshop and seemed to do very little except keep her eyes on me.

She seemed to be listening to every word I spoke with an uncanny ease.

At first, I thought she was bored. Then I thought that perhaps she didn't like what she was hearing or probably knew much more than I did. It was intimidating and scary. Curious, I walked up to her and expressed my concerns. She smiled, held up the Mind Map® book and her notes in a Mind Map® form. Later in the session, she shared with us the rationale and the benefits of the technique. I went home that night and did some research, called up some friends, and was intrigued enough to spend days and weeks learning more about it. In a matter of weeks I started applying the technique and soon became addicted. It worked fabulously! Today, I apply it for reading, researching, writing, during meetings, and for public speaking.

This is how I define Mind Mapping®: a colorful, two-dimensional, quick representation of your ideas, knowledge, and feelings.

The rationale behind Mind Mapping® is that our senses take in a lot of information, and all this input generates responses, ideas, and opinions that cannot be expressed vocally or written down as quickly as they occur. For example, if 10 ideas flash through our minds then we may only be able to express only half of them verbally and less than a quarter in writing. Mind Mapping® provides the answer to this malady: It is like a thought-grabber with eight or ten sets of limbs.

Capturing your thoughts quickly gives you time to analyze and qualify them later. This makes your thinking process more effective. Putting down thoughts in images and colors also enhances retention and invites the creative, right side of your brain to come and play!

How to create a Mind Map®

- Draw an image of your topic using three colors at the center of the paper positioned horizontally.
- Make the central image a representation of the topic. Use images rather than words.
- Draw the main, appealing ideas as thick branches coming
- 12 from the central image.
- Whenever possible, use different color themes for different branches. This will help you segregate and qualify ideas later.
- Maintain one word per branch and keep that word on top of the branch.

- Add images wherever you can instead of words.
- Add arrows between images and branches and ideas expressing relationships or commonalities among the ideas.
- Flow with abandon. Do not judge your thoughts. Grab your ideas first and qualify them later.
- Use capital letters, print, and be creative with your Mind Maps®.

Reading a Mind Map®

A Mind Map® is drawn from the center going outwards and read from the outside going inwards. The primary branches form the main points and the secondary and tertiary branches form the sub-headings or points. The branch and its sub-branches are read flexibly. Read clockwise and then convert single words into simple sentences as you go. Structure, sequence, and polishing off the language in the complete text can be done later.

Benefits of Mind Mapping®

- Noting and reading only relevant words save time.
- Reviewing is graphical and can be done at a glance.
- Concentration on real issues is enhanced.
- Key words are easily discernible since they are placed according
- To importance for easier recall.
- Clear and appropriate associations are made between key words.
- The brain finds it easier to accept and remember the visually stimulating, multi-colored, multi-dimensional Mind Maps® rather than monotonous, boring linear notes.
- While Mind Mapping®, one is constantly on the verge of new realizations; this encourages a continuous and potentially endless flow of thought.
- The Mind Map® works in harmony with the brain's natural desire for completion or wholeness.

- By constantly utilizing both the logical left and the creative right side of the brain, the mind becomes increasingly alert and receptive.

Over the years, as an ardent "Mind-Mapper," I have come to realize that Mind-Mapping my ideas and emotions helps me look at them through a deeper, more colorful perspective. Mind- Mapping my ideas and letting them percolate for a while allows my subconscious to kick-in and gently delete what is unnecessary, enhance and internalize what is useful and good. The process also increases my faith in the value of the material and confidence in my own self.

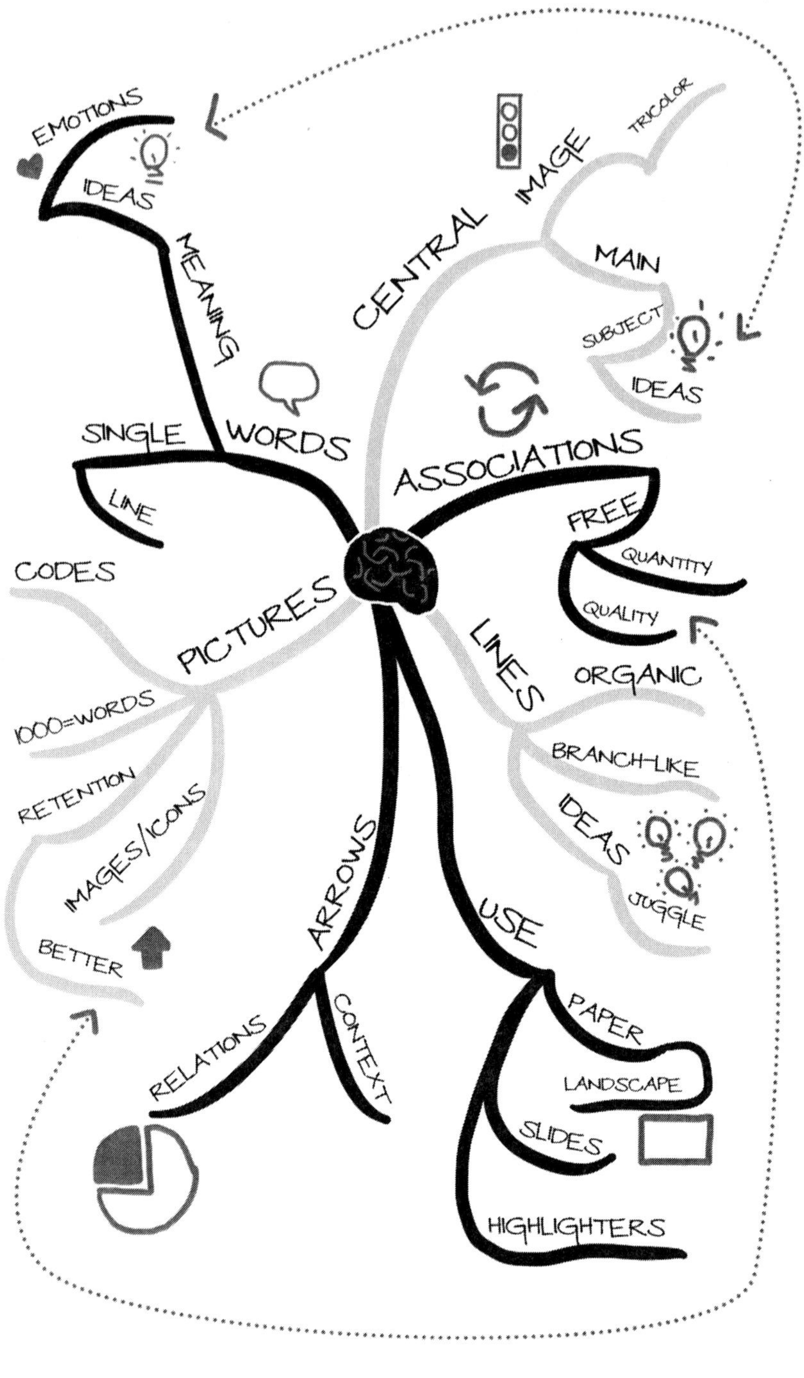

WORDS
SINGLE
LINE
MEANING
EMOTIONS
IDEAS
CENTRAL IMAGE
TRICOLOR
MAIN
SUBJECT
IDEAS
ASSOCIATIONS
FREE
QUANTITY
QUALITY
LINES
ORGANIC
BRANCH-LIKE
IDEAS
JUGGLE
USE
PAPER
LANDSCAPE
SLIDES
HIGHLIGHTERS
ARROWS
RELATIONS
CONTEXT
PICTURES
CODES
1000=WORDS
RETENTION
IMAGES/ICONS
BETTER

Knowing Thyself

The image of myself which I try to create in my own mind in order that I may love myself is very different from the image which I try to create in the minds of others in order that they love me.

- W. H. Auden

The moment you take center stage, you become the heart and soul of all the entities present in the room. Having a clear understanding and consciousness of where you come from, what your beliefs are, and what makes you tick will help you become real about the things you profess.

It is said that a person's physiology, body language, and non- verbal expressions tell more than his words. If you believe that the world is a tough place to live in then it will show through your physiology and manners. If, on the other hand, you believe that life is fun and that the world is a great place, then the audience will consciously or unconsciously see through you. An honest appraisal of your own view of the world will help you adjust your behavior and manners while speaking to an audience.

Many of us take ourselves too seriously. We tend to become extremely conscious of how we look, who we are, and the positions that we hold. As public speakers, once we get up on stage, we put all this and our real selves under sharp scrutiny. This can make us feel so vulnerable that we tend to respond defensively in a non-verbal way, and often, verbally by using the wrong choice of words.

In one of my workshops, the CEO of a mid-sized company stood up to do a presentation. He had prepared well and the audience was aware of his status. He had a clear and commanding voice, but he lacked smoothness and flow when he moved from one concept to another. He was aware of this shortcoming and tried to cover it up by appearing powerful and imposing. As he was about to speak, the waiters in the function room started adjusting the room lights for his visuals.

There were many lights and switches and the waiters created a minor commotion. The delay and the disturbance caused him to lose his composure and he snapped at the waiters, "Can you keep that down and hurry up!" That did it! Though the speaker addressed his irritation towards the waiters, the audience felt rebuked too. He lost control over himself and the audience unconsciously labeled him as a person with low levels of patience and politeness.

We later got together and I gently brought up the incident. He realized his error and agreed that the tension in his composure came from fear and trying to pretend that none existed. He agreed that had he been more at ease with his personality and his prepared materials, he probably would have handled the situation better by using the moment to create humor and win the hearts of his listeners.

As a public speaker, you must take the craft of preparing and delivering a speech seriously, but you must also develop the grace to take yourself and your shortcomings lightly. Learn to focus on your message and less on your fragile ego.

Analyzing Audience Needs

I happen to feel that the degree of a person's intelligence is directly reflected by the number of conflicting attitudes she can bring to bear on the same topic.

– Lisa Alther, Kinflicks

One way to define public speaking and oral presentations is to analyze the word "presentation." "Presentation" stems from the word "present," meaning to bring forth, to give, or to show. It is also a synonym for the word "gift." In essence, a presentation is a "gift" you give to an audience. I am sure you must have spent long hours pondering and planning a gift you want to give someone. You want a gift that would be worthwhile, valuable, and immensely pleasing to the recipient.

Think about the steps you take in giving the perfect gift. The steps you usually take are:

- You get to know the recipient and understand their desires.
- Once you grasp what they want and need, you begin to hunt for the gift that would please them.
- After you have acquired the gift, you take pains in wrapping it attractively in a way that it will surprise and delight the recipient.
- You finally deliver the gift with warmth, confidence, and style.

In the same manner, public speaking is more about the recipients than the speaker or his presentation. If we genuinely care about our audience and give their needs special attention, it will become natural for us to easily please them.

The process is simple. These are the questions you need to answer to analyze audience needs:

- Who are they?
- Who sent them to listen to you?
- Did they come to listen to you out of their own choice? Why?
- What is it that they need to know, understand, or learn?
- What is their educational and work background?
- What age group, gender, and nationality do they belong to?
- What are their specific objectives?
- What is their stock knowledge and experience on the subject?

- How are you qualified to fulfill their expectations and desires?

Following the above method before your speaking event will help create presentations that are clear, concise, and relevant.

Researching Subject Matter

I generally start by taking stock of what I personally know about the subject matter. Obviously, it is not possible to know everything about every subject matter on earth.

Take, for example, rocket science. I have no idea what rocket science is all about, but I do know what a rocket is and what science is.

A rocket is a fuel-powered projectile that shoots into the sky with smoke billowing out from behind it. Science, on the other hand, is the study of how things work, produce, or come about. Rocket science, therefore, must be the study of the how, why, and what about rockets. Right?

"Right!" You say. But what does that prove? Well, it proves one thing: Most of us know a little something about everything in life and that is the point from where we can start our research about a subject.

We must then take this point, consider it the "center" of our thought, and then, as in Mind Mapping®, go outwards. We start from what is known, and then go into the unknown.

Here are some simple steps to follow:

- Mind Map® all that is in your mind as raw data.
- Start talking to family and friends and see what tips and information you can get and add it in.
- Approach teachers, colleagues, and business associates for other input and add it in.

- Tap into your local library for more comprehensive information.
- Use the Internet to get a broader perspective and then you can start narrowing down your topic.
- Interview competition, specialists, or individuals known for their expertise in that field of study.
- Take notes, do more Mind Mapping®. Collect clippings and other materials that you feel are relevant to your subject matter.

Do not, I repeat, do not at this stage start analyzing and judging the relevance of the information that you gather. Just collect a lot of information from as many sources as possible. Do not try to start writing down your speech or presentation at this stage. Gather your information first and let it come together naturally.

The human brain has the capacity to intuitively select, discern, and arrange needed information at the subconscious level. The activity in your mind – subconscious and conscious – is like that of a defragmentation tool on your personal computer. The brain, without any special effort, is defragmenting and putting things in order.

Therefore, at this stage, don't give it any commands that may conflict with its natural process.

After you feel that you have covered sufficient ground, pick up and select what appeals to you most. Remember the ideas from FORCE? Your mind will naturally find relevance, association, and outstanding elements in the material you've covered. Using what you have picked up, create a lengthy first draft of your presentation. We will talk about how to refine, structure, and polish your draft in Chapter 4.

Researching Existing Knowledge

From infancy to adulthood we learn millions of things using all our senses. These millions of things accumulated in the storehouse of our brains become our resource and personality and we become them. In fact, there are schools of thought that believe we start learning and storing information from the time we are in our mother's wombs.

People's knowledge, perceptions, and traits come from varied sources and environments. Some are similar and some are different. Thus we become unique personalities and individuals.

Similarly, practical knowledge about any field or subject matter differs from one person to another. The ways ideas are processed, analyzed, and expressed are unique to each person. A speaker benefits from the process of assimilating the wide variety of thought about a subject matter and adds more to it with new research.

Several years ago, when I had just hit the speaking circuit, I was invited to speak for a local chapter of the Rotarians. I called my host and asked what he wanted me to talk about. He was surprised.

> *"Are you not a speaker? Don't you have a speech?"*
> *"Yes, I am a speaker and I generally speak about speaking," I replied.*

On the telephone, I could almost hear his brain circuits clicking away in confusion. Moments later, he recovered and said, "Okay, speak about anything you like."

Obviously, in my early speaking days, I was hungry for work and took up the challenge of speaking for 30 minutes about "anything."

Without a script or a plan, I arrived at the Rotary meeting an hour before the meeting started. I met every member of the club who walked in that evening. I shook hands, chatted with each of them, asked questions, and took notes. I made jokes about the weather, the traffic, business, and aging gracefully. In that one hour, my hosts were not aware that I had finished doing a simple analysis of my audience and the subject of my speech, "Challenges and Chances after Mid-life: A Rotarian's Perspective."

For the next thirty minutes, I stood up and told them what I thought about the weather, the traffic, business, and aging gracefully. All points I made were from a Rotarian's point of view. I was telling them things that were relevant to them and things that they looked forward to. I talked about aging, their fears, and their individual idiosyncrasies. I had them thinking, feeling, and rolling in the aisles with laughter.

I had given them nothing that they hadn't given me. I was lucky that the topic was "anything." That day, I learned a valuable lesson: Your audience wants to hear about things relevant to them more than whatever your subject matter expertise might be.

Whether you are profiling your audience or researching the subject matter, please do look for emotional anecdotes. These, when added to all the research, will form the second layer for the Heart of Public Speaking.

Keeping an Eye on Humor

"Among those whom I like or admire, I can find no common denominator, but among those whom I love, I can; all of them make me laugh."

- W. H. Auden

Remember when you were a school kid and had to walk in line to get to your classroom?

Remember the time when you wore something radical and let your hair grow and were scoffed at for doing so?

That's about the same time the world and the system started taking away the fun from your life.

Yes, conditioning and discipline are needed in life. But every now and then we need to peep into the flip side of things to get a better perspective of who we are and what our work is all about. Looking at the lighter side becomes de-stressing and therapeutic, and it increases our openness to new ideas.

Imagine a room full of listeners with mindsets of their own staring at you and daring you to change their perspectives. Picture yourself telling them something that they already know. That room is charged with tension and hostility. The solution to banishing such resistance is humor.

Laughter succeeds in cutting down anxiety. It breaks the ice between you, the speaker, and the audience. The question then arises: What kind of humor? When exactly is the time and place to add fun and how should it be presented?

The kind of humor I personally like is home-brewed, situational, and self-inflicted. Any flip point of view about the place, the surroundings, the speaker, or the topic of the speech would be relevant and inoffensive. This kind of humor is not directed towards any class, creed, or community.

The placing of the humor is also extremely important. Humor should not be put into a speech because it is the trend or because all the books on presentation skills and public speaking say so.

Humor should be put in to build rapport and camaraderie and to expose the human side of the speaker, the audience, and the subject at hand.

Humorous statements work best when they create an element of surprise and give the minds of the listeners a sudden twist. Humor should be delivered in places and moments where it is least expected.

I once attended a workshop on comedy by a troupe of Shakespearean dramatists. The exercises were simple and easy but they worked very well because they all had an element of surprise and shock, and they dealt with the existence and acceptance of human frailty and absurdity. There were exercises that included slips of the tongue, unintentional puns, exaggerations, underplay of words, and incongruousness of words to facial expressions.

Here is a sample speech with a large dose of humor in it. It is an introduction of the Commissioner of Customs, Antonio Bernardo of the Philippines to a group of businessmen. I was the introducer and the audience knew me very well. In my talk I claim to be "innocent" and had "blue eyes" while the audience knew otherwise. Adding in these unnecessary exaggerations made them laugh and helped ease the atmosphere of a much too serious business meeting.

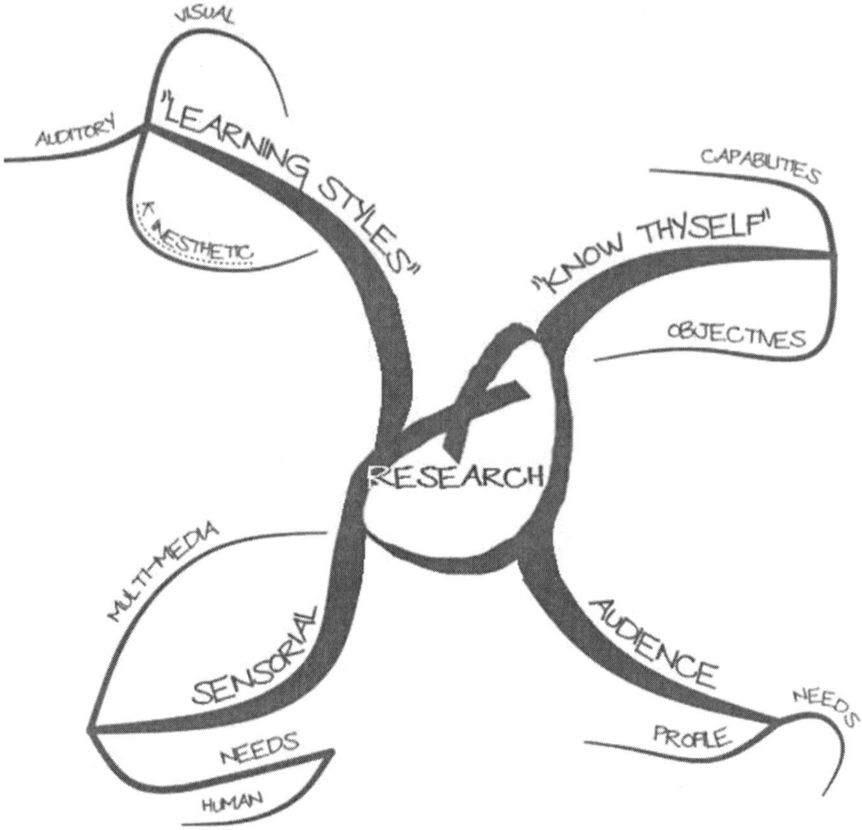

The second layer to the HeART of Public Speaking makes up for the essentials you must research and prepare for before writing and constructing your speech.

AN INTRODUCTION: CUSTOMS COMMISSIONER, ANTONIO BERNARDO

One of the things I believe is that "first impressions" are the best impressions that we have of others.

A few minutes ago, when I laid my deep, blue, innocent eyes upon our chief guest today, these were my spur-of-the-moment impressions of him:

He was young, good-looking and healthy; a combination like that is usually accompanied by a young and healthy mind. A person like that is generally hardworking, honest, wholesome, inspiring, and filled with positive personal and social values.

After I had these "first impressions" about him, I took a look at his résumé which proved my assumptions about him were true!

It is not possible to cover his whole list of achievements but let me list three of his best academic achievements.

He was Class Valedictorian, Don Bosco Technical sometime in the late 1970's.

He was Class Valedictorian, Ateneo University in the early 1980's. And he was the 2nd Placer out of 2,824 examinees at the Bar Exams in 1988.

And I also list three of his professional achievements in recent years that are very impressive.

He has been Undersecretary and Chief of Staff at the Department of Finance and the Department of Energy. Of course, not at the same time!

He has been the Officer-In-Charge at the Social Security System. And he has been Special Assistant to the Chairman at the National Power Corporation.

In fact, the moment we shook hands, the first few words he uttered to me were an articulation of his visions and plans for the Bureau of Customs and the country.

I don't like to make assumptions about people, but of all the impressions I had about our chief guest, none were wrong. I was absolutely right!

I therefore invite our Guest of Honor to come up to the lectern and to leave a first and a lasting impression on all of us with:

His good looks!
His youth and healthfulness!
And his desire to be hardworking, honest, wholesome, inspiring - and a visionary!

Ladies and Gentlemen; I take special pride in giving you the Commissioner of Customs, Mr. Antonio Bernardo of the Philippines!

As you may have realized, the humor in this introduction is mild, contextual and therefore pleasing to the audience. Humor, as Stephen Leacock, states, is "The kindly contemplation of life's incongruities and the artistic expression thereof." Humor is the disruption of logic and the exaggeration of the irregular which, in turn, creates a derailment of the listener's thinking process, making them laugh. An audience which laughs listens well, and an audience that listens well is also easily persuaded.

Therefore, whenever and wherever possible, sprinkle all your talks with an abundance of light-hearted, easy and relevant humor. Use canned jokes only if you do not have anything that you think is relevant. Otherwise, highlight light discussions you may have had earlier with members of the audience, talk about funny experiences on the way to the event, share personal flaws and failures in a comic way and always leave your audiences happier than they were before.

1.0 Insights on Researching for a Speech

1.1 People absorb and retain information in different ways.

1.2 People absorb and retain things that

- they see, hear, or experience First
- they see, hear, or experience Often
- they can Relate to
- are Catchy
- they see, hear, or experience at the End.

1.3 The higher the number of sensory inputs, the better the acceptance, absorption, and retention of new information.

1.4 Mind Mapping® taps into the non-judgmental, creative side of thinking and researching.

1.5 Analyze audiences before starting your research. This way you will know what to focus on.

1.6 Find out how much you personally know about the subject matter and then add in new information and concepts to your research.

1.7 Humor is critical in breaking the ice and creating rapport with the audience. Use humor that is light, relevant, and inoffensive.

1.0 Exercises

1. List at least three benefits that excellence in public speaking can bring about in your personal development.

2. List at least three areas that you believe are your strengths in public speaking.

3. List at least three areas that you would like to improve in your public speaking skills.

4. While doing research, answer the following questions:

 4.1 Who is the speech being prepared for?

 4.2 Why is the speech being prepared for them?

 4.3 What are the objectives that need to be achieved in the presentation?

4.4 When and where is the speech or presentation to be delivered?

4.5 How much time and how many resources will you be given?

5. To increase rapport with my audience, how exactly do I plan to make my listeners laugh while I am discussing serious matters? List at least 3 ideas.

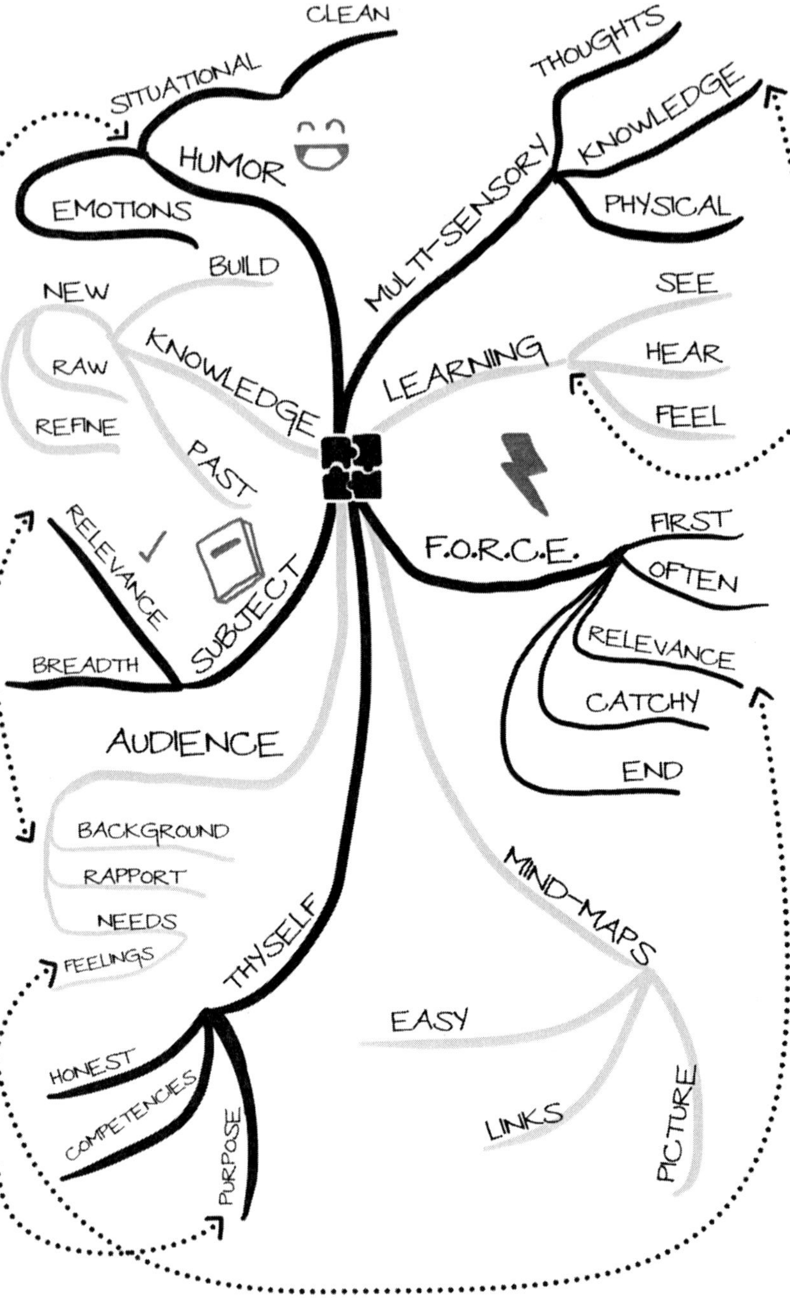
HUMOR
CLEAN
SITUATIONAL
EMOTIONS
MULTI-SENSORY
THOUGHTS
KNOWLEDGE
PHYSICAL
KNOWLEDGE
BUILD
NEW
RAW
REFINE
PAST
LEARNING
SEE
HEAR
FEEL
SUBJECT
RELEVANCE
BREADTH
F.O.R.C.E.
FIRST
OFTEN
RELEVANCE
CATCHY
END
AUDIENCE
BACKGROUND
RAPPORT
NEEDS
FEELINGS
MIND-MAPS
EASY
LINKS
PICTURE
THYSELF
HONEST
COMPETENCIES
PURPOSE

Chapter Two
Planning for a Speech

General Eisenhower used to demonstrate the art of leadership with a simple piece of string.
He would put it on a table and say "Pull it and it will follow you wherever you wish.
Push it and it will go nowhere at all."

- Author Unknown

Visualizing the End

You are now conversant with some of the elements of public speaking and have a general understanding of how the human mind works.

You have learned how to research a speech from all sides and analyze audiences and their needs, and you have also reflected on your own personality and capabilities.

While researching, you have spent several hours or days letting your mind percolate different ideas for the topic. You have studied the functions of the brain and how it builds memory and links information to existing knowledge, and how the new knowledge you are acquiring builds and grows.

All these permutations and combinations happen silently in the brain on a conscious level and at times on the subconscious. Your mind is filling up gaps. It seeks relevance and builds context. The brain chooses and gathers information that will suit and appeal to the target audience. It will choose and gather information that will match your personality.

Now is the time to start projecting yourself into the hour when you will be making that presentation. Imagine yourself up on the podium discussing your topic. See yourself speaking confidently, clearly, and eloquently. Visualize the room, the lights, the people, and your co-speakers. Let this vision become your goal and see yourself achieving it.

Do this often and let this visualization be in color and dynamic. By the time you really take the stage, you will have already mentally lived that moment many times over in a positive manner.

When you visualize success, you will achieve success. It is like a tennis player who serves the ball with a positive vision of landing every ball in a strategic spot on the opposite side. The tennis player does exactly that every time he serves. But when that player worries about getting his ball snagged in the net, then that is exactly what happens!

Your mind tunes in and chooses the physical and the concrete. When you fearfully tell yourself, "Oh, please don't let it hit the net again!" your mind hears and accepts the word "net" more than the word "don't." On the other hand, if you were to tell yourself, "I am going to hit every ball into the opposite court," then that is what the mind hears, believes, and instructs the limbs to follow with precision. Stay positive, visualize a successful end, and that is exactly what you will achieve.

Here is an exercise that will solidify your visualized ending into a reality:

Imagine that several days have passed since your successful speech. Write a letter to a close friend recounting the glorious details of your performance. Describe how energetic you felt before speaking, how eloquent you were, and how your audience smiled, laughed, loved your speech, and cheered you on for more.

Mention how enthusiastic and informative the open forum was and how several people congratulated you for your wit, brilliance, and wisdom after the speech.

You may not mail that letter, but I assure you the exercise works and helps you stay focused and lets your imagination influence your reality.

The Persuasive Speech

Persuasive speeches always have one or more of these objectives: to sell a product or a service, to defend a position, to promote a project, to change opinions, or to inspire a group of people.

Examples of persuasive presentations: sales presentations, campaign or political speeches, speeches for religious and social groups.

The basic idea behind a persuasive speech is to make others believe what you, the speaker believes in.

Persuasive speeches are extremely demanding of the speaker since they are about changing attitudes, opinions, or social structures.

Persuasive speeches have to be structured in such a way that they start from what is known and acceptable to what is yet unknown and should be accepted. The premise should be laid down early or woven into the theme so that the change of mindset happens subtly at the subconscious level.

Every fact, example, and argument must relate and resonate towards the objectives the speaker has in mind. Strong arguments supported by good examples make the speech effective and full of impact. Persuasive speeches are "hot" speeches that stir the passions of all parties involved.

To prepare speeches that are persuasive and motivating, take note of the following elements:

- Know your audience and research their background thoroughly.

- Understand their mindsets and their opinions on your product, service, or proposal.
- Come from a position of credibility. Provide real value about your product, service, or proposal.
- Give real life examples that are testimonies to your product, service, or proposal.
- Be clear and concrete in explaining the benefits of your position.
- Be clear, precise, and absolutely thorough about what you want your listeners to do after hearing your speech.

- During the presentation, speak easily and build rapport and camaraderie.
- Be a pull-seller rather than a pushy salesperson. Show your listeners the wisdom in buying your product, service, or proposal.
- Build belief and faith in your product, service, or proposal and then seek commitment.
- Answer questions courteously and always stay on track with your objectives.

Persuasive presentations are the key to personal success and achieving leadership positions in life.

The Informative Speech

The Informative Speech consists of a list of facts or dates that are logically arranged and structured and easy to follow. Examples of informative speeches are book reports, business reports, and technical briefings. Informative speeches need to be clear in their objectives. They are crisp and concise in structure. It is best to use the multi-sensory approach in communicating information or data.

Use visuals, sounds, samples, and other presentation aids. It is also advisable to show the relevance and association of facts.

All repetition in informative speeches helps enhance the absorption, retention, and the easy recall of data.

To make informative speeches relevant, effective, and interesting, take the following steps:

- Research your facts and data well.
- Polish and refine your speech to cut down to the essentials.
- Enumerate the points you are making in a sequence.
- Be logical and structured.
- Support with statistics, facts, figures, and visuals.
- Speak in an even, clear, and interesting manner.
- Wherever possible, inject a little humor to take the weariness away from dry, plain, and data-intensive talks.

The Entertaining Speech

There was no respect for youth when I was young,
and now that I am old there is no respect for age.
I missed it coming and going.

– J.B. Priestly

Unlike the Persuasive Speech, which changes mindsets, and the Informative Speech, which transfers knowledge, an Entertaining

Speech makes the speaker and the listener feel good about life and themselves.

An Entertaining Speech is light, fun, and gracious. Speeches in the form of toasts, roasts, stand-ups, and after-dinner chats are examples of entertaining speeches. An Entertaining Speech sells or promotes happiness and gratitude.

Still, as speeches go, the Entertaining Speech needs a good opening, a good closing, and a fun-filled relevant middle. The closing need not be a summary or a call for action, but it needs to end on a high and happy note.

The elements of an entertaining speech are:

- Several humorous anecdotes about the characters involved.
- Dialogues between characters.
- A "flip" look at serious things.
- Preferably spoken in the first person and told in the present tense.
- Ideas and suggestions in the speech should be quick on the set-up and quicker on the punch.
- Several voice modulations should be part of the delivery style.
- It should not be very long.

The speaker also needs to open up and get close to the audience mentally, physically, and emotionally.

Here is an example of a pointless but completely entertaining speech. I present it here with apologies to all the women of the world.

Analogies and Anecdotes

Analogies are comparisons of two things that are alike in some ways and different in others. They are explanations of ideas and concepts in a language, listeners can understand and relate to. Analogies increase the audience's level of interest since they create more than one image of reference.

For example: Imagine that your brain is like a computer. It has a long-term permanent memory just like the hard disk, and it has a short term, quick memory like the desktop memory of a computer.

Analogies are very useful public speaking tools and can be used to increase the level of participation and fun in presentations.

Anecdotes or stories are the most exciting elements that a public speaker can put in his presentations. They give a touch of reality to facts and figures. They are interesting, relevant, and have a sequential flow of concepts and incidents.

Anecdotes involve the listeners more because they delve into a speaker's personal knowledge and experiences. Anecdotes also create multiple contexts for enhanced understanding of what is being presented.

In public speaking, anecdotes need to be detailed yet brief. If you are using old, known stories then you need to give them a modern twist and also add a personal touch.

Several years ago, a friend of mine was planning to use the well-known story of "Casey at the Bat" for an Asian audience.

I recommended to my speaker friend that he stay with the gist and value of the story, but change the main characters name to something Asian like "Chong," and create an Asian scenery in describing the playing field and the crowds. He did so and got a hearty response from his Asian audience.

Anecdotes work best when they describe our own experiences and feelings. They become fun when we talk about our own misinterpretations and foibles. Anecdotes need to describe the time, location, and the characters involved. They should be told from the perspective of a single protagonist and must be novel yet familiar.

If our anecdotes have dialogues between two or more characters, altering your voice for each character will enhance the presentation. It will make the story and the characters believable.

You can also step out of the story every now and then for dramatic effect, relating to it from the listeners' point of view.

Anecdotes, like a good joke, must be clean, positive, and have a message instead of a punch line. They should always bring the audience's attention back to your main topic.

Openings, Bodies and Closings

> *"Where shall I begin, please Your Majesty?" he asked. "Begin at the beginning," the King said gravely, "and go on till you come to the end, then stop."*
>
> **- Lewis Carroll**

The opening, the body, and the closing determine the major elements of a speech's structure. Speeches need to be structured, linear, and smooth to transfer ideas efficiently and effectively.

The opening, which establishes rapport and the premise of the talk, also reveals the personality of the speaker. It takes up the first few moments of the speech and helps the audience determine their attitude towards the speech and the speaker. Here, first impressions and the Law of Primacy take effect.

Therefore, the opening has to be very carefully planned, prepared, and delivered. It can be compared to your first date with the person you want to marry. Your first night out must be filled with attentiveness, honesty, and wit.

Openings with a joke, quote, or a startling piece of news are good only if they are:

- Relevant to the subject or the topic of the speech.
- Suitable to the audience and the occasion.
- Something personal and suitable to the speaker's style.

All of the above should resonate with the atmosphere, the mood, and the people involved in the speaking event.

Openings also need to be short and outstanding. The opening is a picture of things to come and of the main points the speaker plans to present.

- Ask a rhetorical question. Asking a question arouses the listener's interest and sets him up in a receptive mode.
- State a startling fact or a statistic. Something like, "Last year, just in the city of New York, 700 people died from choking on chicken bones!" This perks up the audience's attention and arouses their curiosity.
- Relate a personal story or an anecdote. Personal experiences are more convincing and interesting because they are backed up by a real visual: you!
- Recite a poem or a quote. Everyone loves rhyme and rhythm and hearing what authorities or celebrities have to say.
- Present a sample or a visual: A picture speaks a thousand words and a sample perks up the Kinesthetic learners amongst the audience. It also helps the speaker have an object of reference for his talk.

The body is crucial and is held together by a good opening and a closing. If openings can be compared to the first night out with the love of your life, then be aware that the main body of the speech carries as much importance as the maintenance and sustenance of a life-long relationship.

The body needs to be interesting, invigorating, and extremely interactive. It should have direction, purpose, and completeness without being wordy. The body should have clarity, sequence, and a lot of “give and take.” The life and spirit of the speech need to be within the body.

Finally, the closing provides a recollection of the essential parts of the body. It makes a reference to the opening or the premise of the speech and provides definitive directions for the action to be taken by the listeners. The closing also needs to close on a high, inspirational note, just as a mature relationship that looks forward to its golden years with hope and happiness.

- Summarize the main points: A summary is a review and repetition. It refreshes everything that has occurred and repackages the learning.
- Recite a poem or state a quote: Again if there is a quote that nicely represents all the points made then it will have a pleasant and a lasting effect on the memories of the listeners.
- Leave them with a question to think about: This works well at the subtle level and it gives you a chance to achieve your personal objectives some other time.
- Call for action: State exactly what you want the listeners to do after you have stated your proposals. State them in “do” terms.
- Always end on a high and motivational note; as public speakers we are leaders. It behooves us to inspire people to be better. Unless, of course, you really intend to leave people in an introspective and serene mood.

Now, the analogy to a loving couple that I’ve created in the last few paragraphs may have made you smile! What I have done is illustrate my topic by giving it a slightly unrealistic but humorous comparison. Such hooks and transitions induce interest and participation. Humor that is pleasant and woven into the main content becomes a part of the tapestry over which the speech is laid out. This humor does not have to be political, religious, or racial. The subtler and more surprising it is, the more it will be appreciated and enjoyed.

Humor, as also discussed in "Chapter 3: Writing A Speech" must be situational, inoffensive, even self-deprecating for effect for use whenever and wherever possible.

Structuring your Speech through Basic Formats

As discussed earlier, all speeches consist of an opening, body, and closing. The internal formats in the opening, body, and closing are further made up of elements such as opinions, reasons, research, examples, benefits, proposals, stories, messages, and applications.

These elements help build a speech that ranges from the simple to the complex.

The quantity of information and value a speaker puts into the speech depends on the speaker's knowledge, the background of his listeners, as well as the time allotted for that speech.

Before you start planning and writing down your speech, you need to understand certain formats and structures. These formats and structures make up all the work that goes behind great performances that seem smooth, flawless, and exciting. They will refine and shape all that is going on in your mind about your future presentation.

During the 2000 U.S. Presidential elections, C-Span featured a televised debate between candidates George Bush and then Vice President, Al Gore. Several years prior to this debate, I had watched Al Gore perform, and he seemed stuffy, dry, and uptight. But during this debate, Al Gore was smooth, precise, and polite. His opinions were clear, supported by reason, and backed up by examples. He often concluded his arguments with reiteration and rephrased his opinion for effect. My assumption was that he had undergone a massive amount of coaching by public speaking experts and was using several combinations of formats as described in the next paragraph.

These formats and their combinations make wonderful, well-crafted speeches that sound natural and confident. Professional public speakers intuitively and habitually apply such formats in most presentations they make. As you apply these formats to your own presentations, you will also develop a keen ear and eye for these techniques when used by other speakers.

These three formats and a variety of other combinations can be mixed and matched to craft an effective presentation. An example of an effective presentation using OREO + ALA + PAB can be seen in the illustration.

Have a full-fledged presentation can be achieved using these format is illustrated on page 53. This structuring format makes up the third layers in the heart of speaking.

OREO: Opinion, Research, Example and Opinion

Opinion: The cloning of humans is a dangerous endeavor.

Research: There have been many cases where cloning of humans has failed and brought about disastrous results. Genetic modification can be controlled only in the early stages of development but goes amuck after a certain development stage is reached.

Example: Last year in Miami, a perfect human clone was formed. Everything seemed all right for the first nine months. But after that

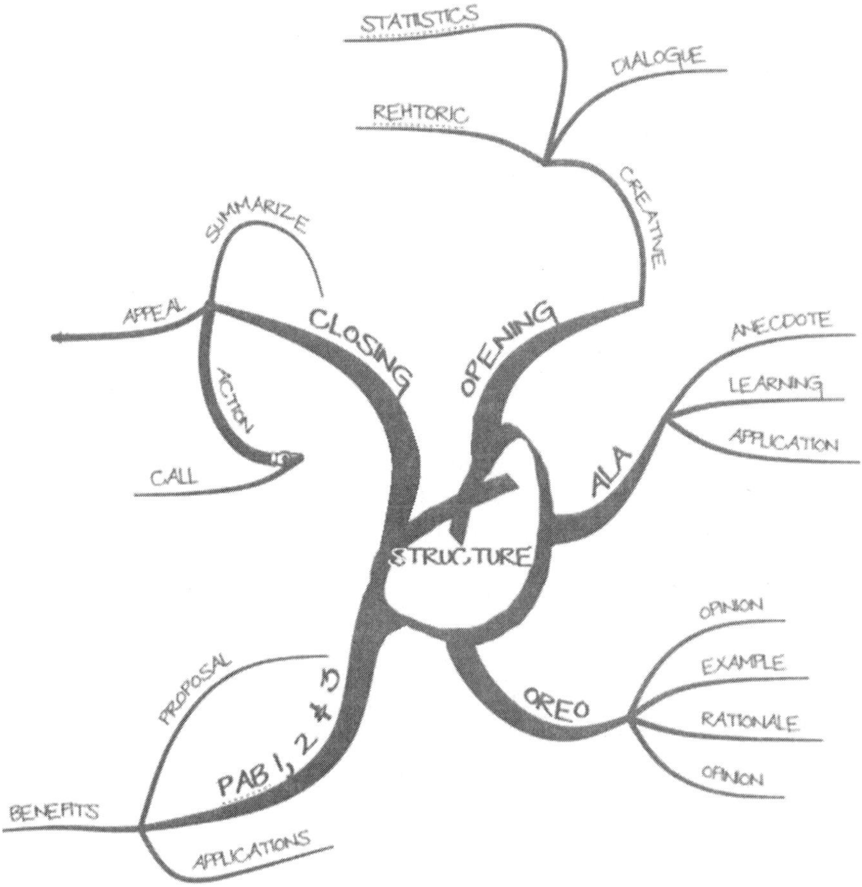

A well-structured speech with planned formats within makes up the third layer to the HeART of Public Speaking.

Note that closing must tie-up well to the opening.

the specimen's skin started wrinkling excessively, and it developed rashes all over its body. In less than a year, the specimen had aged thirty times faster than the natural process.

Opinion: We cannot stress hard enough the negative consequences of human cloning.

ALA: Anecdote, Learning and Application

Anecdote: Last year in Miami, a human was successfully cloned. The scientists behind the successful efforts were very elated, but their elation did not last more than a year. The specimen began to age at an alarming rate: it aged thirty times faster when compared to the natural aging process.

Learning: We feel that scientists today are not equipped with enough knowledge to cope with these repercussions. Any steps taken in this direction would be premature and extremely dangerous.

Application: We have concluded that mankind should stay away from tampering with natural processes in and out of research labs. All our research efforts and funds should be applied to other fields of study.

PAB: Proposal, Applications and Benefits

Proposal: We suggest that you try routing all your e-marketing campaigns through our company for the next 12 months.

Applications: Our e-marketing services will:

- Handle all your e-mail campaigns.
- Keep a log of all responses.
- Carry pictures and your company logo, since it is HTML-based.
- Reach 10,000 recipients per click.
- Constantly update your database.

Benefits: You will have a 40% reduction in e-mailing campaign costs. Your computer time will be cut by half and your marketing reach will double.

Here is a sample speech using the ALA: Anecdote + Learning + Application format.

THE TRANSCENDENTAL VIEW

Why is it that most people treat foreigners differently and jump to conclusions about them? Like the moment I land in the Philippines, people go "Bumbai!"

When I land in India, people go "NRI!" (which means Non Resident Indian, but what they are really implying is "Not Responsible Indian.")

Boy, am I glad I don't travel to a country of cannibals. I am sure the moment they look at me they would go "Food!"

A few months ago, after I finished a 3-day workshop on Leadership & Values at a 5-Star Hotel in New Delhi, dressed in faded jeans and T-shirt, I was paying my bill when I realized I'd been billed 4,500 rupees a night when I clearly remembered the charge being 3,500 rupees a night. The girl at the counter said because I was an NRI, I was billed in U.S. dollars but would have to pay in the local currency purchased at the hotel's dollar selling rate. Strange, but true! "That is the law and nothing can be done about it," she said. I refused to pay and requested to see the manager.

Soon, an oversized Indian in a black suit and tie appeared in front of me. He had gel in his hair, gel on his moustache and gel on his eyebrows. To my query, he repeated the same thing the girl at the counter had told me. It was the law and I had to pay!

"Look," I said. "Let's get three things straight here! One, I generate an income in India; I spend from that money and pay my taxes too! Two, nobody told me about this law when I signed in at 3500

Rupees a night. And three, common courtesy demands that before you take my money you seek my permission!" I was red in the face and loud while Mr. Gel-on-his-Moustache began to get tough and kept repeating that it was the law and I should have known about it.

A crowd began to gather around us. I became conscious of my Fil-American accent, my faded jeans and my tired looks from the last three days of training. Three days of Leadership & Values! Three days of positive thinking and pro-activism and at the end of it I was quarreling with my hosts!

I stopped! I stopped and took in the ludicrous situation.

I stepped back and heard my own heartbeat! I became conscious of my flushed looks and the crowd around me. I slowly transcended out of the scene and began to breathe slowly and let a smile appear on my face. Gently, I said I will accept whatever has to be done.

He saw the change come over my attitude and my whole being. Slowly, his moustache became less stiff. After a long pause, he smiled and then began to speak. "Sir, I need to follow the law and charge you 4,500 Rupees, but because you are a special guest, out of the three nights that you have stayed with us, I am going to let you have one night free."

We looked at each other for a long while. I thanked him, he thanked me, and soon there were smiles all around. The tension disappeared. I paid my bill and as I was about to leave, a smiling bellboy tried to reach for my bag. I yelled at him, "Don't you touch that bag!" He stepped back, shocked and scared. "Just kidding!" I added.

The fact is that when we are in the thick of a problem, all we see is our own point of view and our own ego. In times like this, we need to step back, observe the life around us, and transcend the scene. Seeing the bigger picture and doing an honest appraisal will help us resolve most problems.

The technique of stepping back, taking in the bigger picture, and looking for positives will cut down interpersonal conflicts, reduce unwanted stress, and increase our overall performance and efficiency.

Environmental Factors: Lighting, Acoustics and Room Layout

As a speaker you have a say on the quality of room lighting, acoustics, and layout. Take the opportunity to adjust them to your needs.

Keep in mind that people are multi-sensorial in nature. Some of these senses are consciously controlled while others are reactive and operate on their own. Your audience can give you their eyes and ears, but if the rest of their senses are uncomfortable, they will be distracted and inattentive.

A person sitting in a backless chair will not be much of a listener if, after some time, his back starts screaming for rest. Likewise, a person sitting in a very warm room or in a room that is freezing will not be of much use to you as a listener.

A room that has a substantial number of glass windows is recommended because every now and then your listeners would need to move their eyes away from you. A view of the sky or the landscape keeps them in touch with a pleasant reality while at the same time enjoying your speech. Rooms that are dimly lit create gloominess and discomfort. Rooms that are too bright strain the eyes.

Most convention halls and function rooms are rectangular. Event managers like to keep the podium or the lectern at the narrow end of the room. We are all aware that sound travels in waves and circles away from the source. A speaker placed at the narrow end of a room has to project his voice farther than someone speaking from the wider end of the room.

Sound systems help in magnifying your voice, but they do not help in clarifying, modulating, or making it pleasant to the ear. You need your lungs and your vocal chords for that. Wherever possible, choose to speak from the wide end of the room and see that walls or partitions, and not doors and windows, are behind you. The latter will distract your listeners and your voice will mix with other sounds coming from them.

It is advisable for a speaker to check the sound system before the speaking engagement. There are occasions when halfway through a speech the sound system breaks down or a power failure occurs. Once, I was at a large convention. The cables connected to the speakers at the back of the room were exposed in many places and were sometimes crisscrossing the room under the carpets. When the room filled, someone tripped over a connection and cut off the sound system. Imagine the long agonizing minutes I spent trying to maintain audience attention with just my voice and exaggerated gestures!

Professional speakers are meticulous persons and like to bring down the margin for error as close to zero as possible. One time, I attended a conference to hear Ron Kaufman, the Customer Relationship Management Guru. On the day of the conference, I was the first to arrive at 7:30 a.m. So I went to find a seat in the first row, near the podium. I saw a sprightly man in jeans and T-shirt checking the stage, the lighting, the wiring, the loudspeakers, and flip charts. The man was scurrying about, verifying and checking everything. I kidded him about having to slave so early in the morning for some big-time public speaker and he responded jovially.

An hour or so later, when the audience had come in, I was still in the front seat when the first speaker of the day was announced. A bright-looking young man walked up front with a snap in his stride. It was the same sprightly man I had seen an hour earlier!

He saw my jaw drop as he turned towards me and gave me a double thumbs-up with a huge smile on his face. The "maintenance boy" in ragged jeans I'd seen checking the system earlier was Ron Kaufman himself!

That day, I learned one of the most important lessons in a speaker's life. As a speaker, you are responsible for the quality of your performance. Therefore, you are also responsible for the systems and equipment that help you become a public speaker.

Room Layout

Now that we know the importance of lighting and acoustics to a public speaking event, let's look at how best to lay out the furniture to encourage efficient dialogue, movement, and interaction with your audience. Here are some points you ought to consider:

An ideal seating arrangement allows all listeners to face the speaker and still be spacious.

- The front row should not be too close to you. Listeners seated here will be pressured by the proximity of your presence and your body language. Listeners also know that speakers often call front-rowers for interaction and questions. Not many listeners want that to happen. In small function rooms maintain at least a distance of two steps between you and the seats in the first row. In larger rooms with larger audiences, have all the "backbenchers" come up as close as possible to the stage.

- Do not put chairs and tables too far from the stage. This makes you exert more effort to connect with the backbenchers. As in high school, when not attended to, they will start their own private little conference and disrupt the rapport and connection that you may be working on with the rest of the audience. Keep them close to keep them within the "loop of the magic" you are creating.

- Maintain a generous distance between tables. People like to mix with groups, but they don't like others to eavesdrop or barge into their personal space. Generous aisles and spaces allow listeners to move about easily too. And if you're a speaker who likes to get into the midst of your audience, then the generous space between tables will give you the freedom to do so.

Handling Multimedia and Visuals

Multimedia material or equipment, such as videos or audio equipment, LCD projectors, and computers can support multi-sensorial learning and impart knowledge. But if not handled properly, they can be a major hindrance to audience connectivity and the sensitivity of dialogue a speaker needs to maintain. Make your visuals light, entertaining, colorful, and supportive. Make them pleasant, easy to understand, and visible enough for the backbenchers to see.

Test, rehearse, and synchronize your speech and multimedia sequences several times before presenting. Do not let any of your multimedia special effects become overwhelming. Remember: People have come to hear you speak, not watch a homemade movie.

Here are other suggestions for handling and timing when projecting images and facts on a screen:

- Do not stand in front or cross the light from the projector. This annoys the audience and hampers communication.
- Do not speak to the screen or to the projector. Keep your eyes and your attention on the audience. Your eyes, your expressions, and your body movements should support and elaborate the words and pictures that you put up on the screen. People come in for presentations, talks, and workshops expecting action, dynamism, and participation.
- In an 8 x 11 transparency, follow the 3 x 5 rule: maximum of three lines of approximately five words each.
- If any of your equipment lets you down, do not stomp your feet or use foreign language. Your audience is sensitive and might quickly label you as an easily irritable person.
- Turn off the projector light when it is not in use. You don't want the glare to tire the eyes of the audience and thereby lessen their interest in your talk.

Seminar Materials and Handouts

People love to get their hands on reading materials at conferences because it makes them feel involved. And then there are speakers and trainers who believe that the thicker the seminar kit, the more impressed their audiences will be.

The idea behind a public speaking event is human-to-human interaction. If we wanted a lot of reading material, then a bookstore, not the presentation, would be a better solution.

Here are several tips that will make your handouts useful, and interesting:

- Let the seminar materials have words and ideas other than those that you are going to use in your speech.
- Put simple pointers and facts.
- Provide numerical data, formulas, and illustrations that are not part of your verbal delivery.
- Information in the handout should be minimal. Explain the bulk of the knowledge.

- Make the layout simple, easy to read, and with margins for note-taking.

The correct time for distributing handouts to your participants depends on the content you are providing them.

- Distribute the handouts ahead of time if they contain notes you want them to preview before your presentation, like a background on the topic.
- If exercises and questionnaires are involved, give them out just before the interaction or the question-and-answer session.
- If you are providing supporting material for later reading, distribute them after the presentation.

As much as possible, you do not want the minds of your audience going ahead of you, straying, or lagging behind the concepts presented during the session. Just remember that you are the head, the heart, and the source of humor behind the event. Let that always be the status quo.

Common Speech Structures

Here is a list of speeches that are commonly used in business meetings and conferences. The list below will describe what goes into such speeches. I suggest you take into account audience needs and objectives, and then have a proper opening, body, and closing. Figuring in the principles of FORCE will make your speeches dramatic and memorable.

1. Introducing a Speaker

- Give a background of the speaker and how you know or see him as a person.
- Keep it upbeat, affirmative, and brief.
- Talk about why the speaker's topic is important and how he is qualified to tackle it.
- Close on a high, mention the title and the name of the speaker at the very end.

2. Delivering the Opening Remarks of a Session

- Talk about the importance of the event and how it came about.
- Talk about what the event hopes to achieve.
- Mention the details of the program and the participants.
- Keep the mood upbeat and motivate the audience to partake and participate.

3. Delivering the Closing Remarks of a Session

- Thank all those who helped bring the event together. Make special mention of sponsors, if any.
- State the highlights of the event and their importance.
- State and summarize all the event objectives that were achieved.
- Create a sense of expectancy for all such events in the future.
- Be gracious and end on a very cheerful note.

4. Delivering the Keynote Address

- Talk about the past, the present, and the future of all the issues or topic at hand.
- Include anecdotes that are motivating and extremely vivid.
- Create hope and be a visionary in attitude.
- Describe in detail what efforts are being made to handle the issues at hand and describe strategy and action plans.
- Remember, you are the main event and your topic is the essence of the whole meeting. Be larger than life and take liberties with the material you put into your presentation.

5. Offering a Toast

- A toast praises and puts the one being toasted upon a pedestal.

- A toast can be flowery and humorous. Use quotes, limericks, and poems if you wish.
- Be truthful and yet be very, very brief.
- Raise your glass as you start to speak and take the first sip right after you conclude speaking.
- Look at the recipient as you speak slowly and cheerfully.

6. Roasting Someone

- Include several humorous anecdotes about the one being toasted.
- String together the anecdotes and deliver in a tongue- in-cheek manner.
- Be cautious of being insulting, obnoxious, and politically incorrect.

7. Delivering an Inaugural Speech

- Be humble, thankful, and frank.
- Acknowledge the participation and all the previous input of the audience.
- Seek change and request teamwork.
- Articulate plans and programs and be motivating.
- Close with hope and a call for action.

8. Delivering a Valedictory

- State "where you were" at the beginning and "how far you have come" as a team.
- Mention and describe in details all efforts and input of others.
- Be humble about your own input and be gracious and thankful about the efforts of others.
- Cheerfully invite the next leader to take the team to the next level.

9. Delivering a Status Report

- Be informative yet as brief as possible.
- Submit data and reports in writing, wherever needed.
- State "where we were," "where we are today," and "where we will be going," also known as the Past, Present and Future format.
- Compare and contrast with previous performances.
- Acknowledge expectations, state socio-economic conditions, and highlight achievements.
- Describe strategy and plan of action.
- Speak affirmatively and offer appreciation for all support received.

These nine presentation structures are just a few of the many that we may need to make at work. What is and will always be important is to apply the myriad of suggestions this book recommends and, sometimes, mix your own concoctions, first through effort and eventually through your heart.

2.0 Insights on Planning for a Speech

2.1 Positive visualization of your performance will guarantee good results.

2.2 The body of the speech or the content must be created first, the opening and closing built in later.

2.3 Using anecdotes and creating analogies of personal experience increase the value and impact of the speech.

2.4 Three structural formats that can fit into any classification of speech are:

- OREO
- ALA
- PAB

2.5 The physical structure and atmosphere in a room must always be conducive to the audience's comfort.

2.6 Your visual aids must enhance and support your spoken presentation. They must not be the presentation.

2.7 Depending on their sequence, seminar materials and kits must be given either before, during, or after the presentation.

2.0 Exercises

1. Five ways to open a speech are:

    1.1 Ask a Q_ _ _ _ _ _ _ _ .
    1.2 State a startling F _ _ _ or a S _ _ _ _ _ _ _ _ _ .
    1.3 Relate a personal S _ _ _ _ .
    1.4 Recite a P _ _ _ or a Q_ _ _ _ .
    1.5 Present a S _ _ _ _ _ or a V _ _ _ _ _ .

2. Five ways to close a speech are:

    2.1 S _ _ _ _ _ _ z _ the main points.
    2.2 Call for A _ _ _ _ n.
    2.3 Recite a P _ _ _ or a Q_ _ t _ .
    2.4 Leave them with a Q_ _ s _ _ _ _ to ponder.
    2.5 Always close on a high and on a 67 M _ _ _ v _ _ _ note!

3. What is the optimum number of sentences per 8 x 11 visual and how many words are ideal for a sentence in a visual?

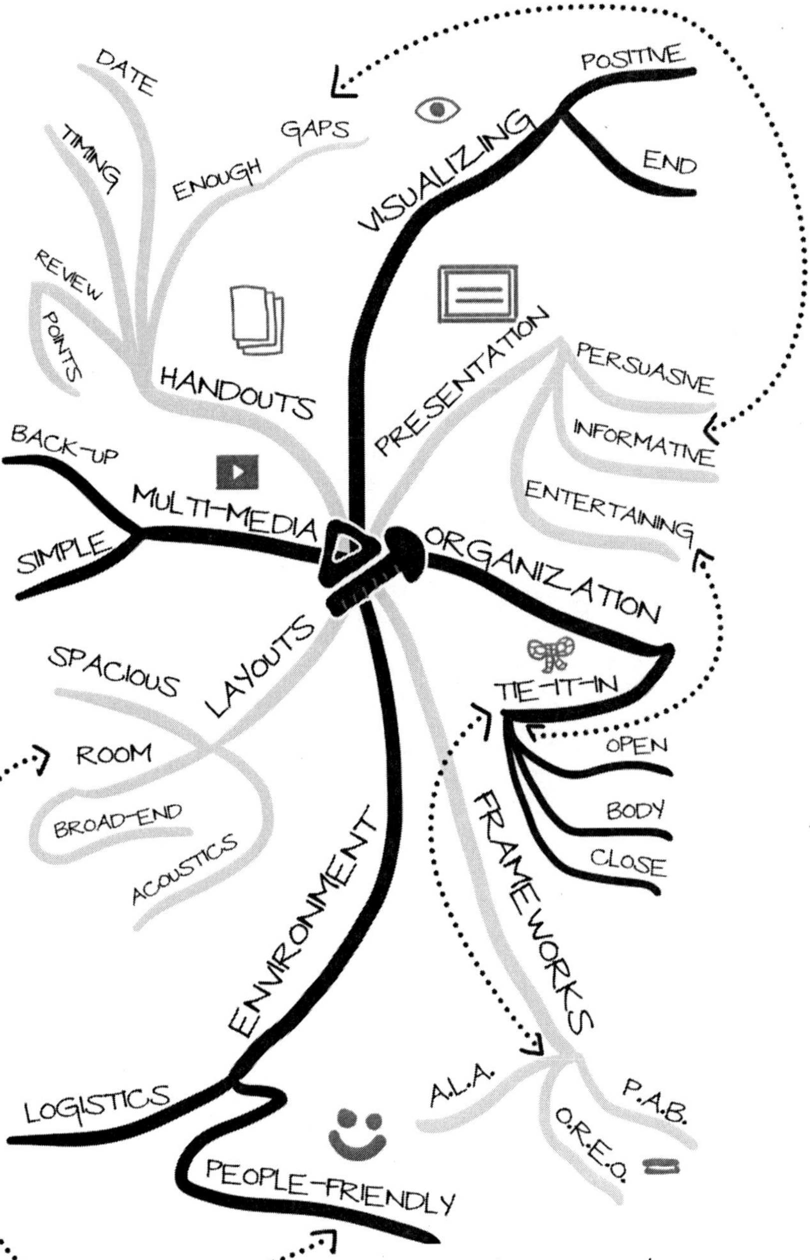

A Mind Map on Planning

Chapter Three
Writing a Speech

If I am to speak ten minutes, I need a week for preparation. If I am to speak for fifteen minutes- three days. If half an hour, two days. And, if for an hour, I am ready now.

- Woodrow Wilson

Minding the Time: Understanding Speaking Speed

There is no speaker in the corporate world that is not time-bound. I would probably do a double flip and a cartwheel if a host told me that I could start and end whenever I wanted and speak as much as my heart desired.

Time represents people-hours, and people-hours are measured by money. Depending on the level of the other speakers and the level of the audience, some of these people-hours can be very expensive. Therefore, we must be extremely time-conscious and time-bound. Using the structure and formatting methods we've just learned, we can also manage speaking time so that we can start and end our presentations with precision.

People have different speaking rates. Fast speakers, like the auctioneers of days gone by, can spew out anywhere from 150 to 200 words per minute in intelligible language. John F. Kennedy was known for being able to speak clearly at the rate of 200 words per minute. Mahatma Gandhi spoke at the rate of 140 words per minute in English as well as in Hindi, his native tongue.

Most people speak at a rate between these two parameters. To find out your speaking rate, take a written speech, count the words, and then read it out loud in your normal speaking rate, monitored by someone with a stopwatch or by a voice recorder. Experiment a few times in your best voice; calculate your words per minute, and then average out your performances. When speaking in public, under pressure, and in the presence of a large audience, allow 20 percent additional time.

This additional 20 percent is a safety measure for slips of the tongue, interjected questions, and/or problems with sound or technical systems.

Once you know your speaking rate, it is easy to develop and write content that will fit your allotted time. Many word processors have a word count feature. Use this feature to measure the length of your first drafts, rewrites, and final presentations. For example, if you are allotted a 20-minute presentation and your speaking rate is 160 words per minute, then a talk of not more than 2,600 words ensures you stay on time.

Keep in mind that people have short attention spans. You and your presentation are not the only inputs their minds are receiving at any given moment. The minds of your audience have other sights, sounds, tastes, and perceptions to process. A straight 40-minute talk is long and demanding for the speaker and his listeners. If your presentation calls for more time, allow for reality checks and variation in delivery styles at least every 20 minutes.

If 30 minutes are allotted to you as a speaker, then the suggested ratios for opening, body, and closing of a speech are: 2 to 4 minutes for the opening, 20 to 25 minutes for the main body, and 3 to 6 minutes for the closing. This kind of time frame allows flexibility and gives space for contingencies or questions.

Clarity, Precision, Relevance, Sequence, and Simplicity

We have already discussed formats and structures and understood the importance of powerful openings, memorable closings, and a well-developed main body of a speech. We have also learned how to insert humorous transitions for a smooth and flowing style.

The traditional way of writing a speech would be to take a slip of parchment, dip the quill into a pot of ink, and start at the top of the page with something like: "Four Score and Twenty Years Ago, Our Forefathers..."

That would be the normal method, and that has its upsides and downsides. All the models and techniques that I have prescribed earlier have been leading us to what I like to call the "Going for the gut of the matter" process.

Let me explain. Starting at the top of the page and starting with the beginning is a very linear way of thinking. It is very left- brained. The tendency with "Four Score and Twenty Years" is to continue with "Four Score and Twenty-One Years," on to "Four Score and Twenty-Two Years Ago," and so on. Your speech may become list-like and have your audiences predicting what you'll say next.

It is perfectly all right to have audience involvement and interest at a high in your presentation, but it can be detrimental to your objectives and performance in general if their minds run ahead of you and away from your speech. There will be times when you want your audience to say, "I know where the speaker is going," but there will be times you would want your audience to be amazed. You do not always want them thinking and saying to themselves, "I know where she is headed; I see all the signs and it's predictable. Ho-hum!"

To maintain audience interest and involvement at a high, learn to inject a little mystery and surprise in your presentations to amaze the audience. You want them to go out enthusing, "That was a good speech! I loved it!"

To achieve this, when writing a speech, do not start from the top or the opening – start with the middle. Yes, go straight to the body. Go for the gut!

Several years ago there was this commercial in the U.S.A. for Burger King– a fast-food chain. The commercial had a muscular, mean-looking, mohawk-haired Mr.T biting into a competitor's cheeseburger and growling into the camera, "Where's the beef?"

If you want your presentation to satisfy and please, then start with the middle, the "gut" or the body of your presentation. Start with the beef, then the spread, lettuce, cheese, pickles, and ketchup. Finally pack the meat into a warm, sesame seed bun. Not only must the "beef" in the middle be juicy and delicious, it should also be nourishing. It must be the "beef" that'll make your audience fulfilled and happy.

Precision

Perfection is achieved, not when there is nothing more to add, but when there is nothing left to take away.

– Antoine de Saint- Exupery

The secret in creating a palatable dish is the quality of the meat. Before evaluating speeches or presentations, a mentor friend of mine, Toastmaster Julia Holz of the ADB, would ask each speaker: "Can you state in just one sentence what you are going to say in your 20-minute speech?"

That question challenged and stupefied many speakers. In this one sentence, she did not seek the title of the speech, but the essential message of the speech. This one-sentence "core" is the foundation of a whole presentation. This should be the starting point of every speech.

This is the heart of your speech. On it you hook all supporting opinions, research, reasons, examples, stories, and facts. All these supporting elements must be turned towards this heart, and must establish the message and the objectives again and again in several ways.

Relevance

The moment we discover this essential core, master the precision required in the message and utilize it; relevance in your speech then becomes easy. Discovering this relevance is achieved through a stringent analysis of objectives.

Let's state these objectives:

- Who is the audience and what do they expect from my presentation?
- How will they respond to my message and apply it?
- What do I plan to achieve in my presentation?
- Has my material been well researched?
- Is it current and verified?
- Will it help the listeners in many ways?
- What is going to be my personal gain?
- Why am I saying the things I say? Do I have any hidden agenda that even I am not conscious of?

Doing this exercise mentally or on paper by using a Mind Map® (discussed in Chapter 2) will redefine your objectives and help you achieve relevance and precision.

Presentations that are too wordy or too detailed get fuzzy in their message. Presentations that are very specific and have just facts and figures do not give us the big picture. The answer lies in telling things in just the right number of straight, direct and well-chosen words.

Sequence

Sequencing your presentation as you are writing it is like taking your audience on a journey from the simple to complex. Sequence is leading your audience from the known to the unknown. Or put differently, from concept to application and practicability of the propositions.

The easier and smoother your presentation is, the more comfortable your audience will be. This sets up the audience for the full impact and appreciation of your presentation. There is an old saying amongst public speakers that goes, "Tell 'em what you are going to tell 'em, tell 'em what you have to tell 'em, and then tell 'em what you have told 'em."

If you are stating an opinion, are you backing it up with reason and examples? If you are relating an anecdote, are you clarifying the learning points and the applications behind it? If you are presenting a proposal, are you communicating the application and benefits to the audience? Are all the elements of speech arranged so listeners can easily follow?

Ask these questions and evaluate your presentation for sequence and structure.

This is a simple route to follow. In the subsequent chapters, we'll use variations of this technique to give your speech added twist and flavor.

Simplicity

Many times, to make a presentation sound more profound than it really is, people use flashy words that complicate the message. A presentation should be created in a language that is as plain as possible.

For example:

Instead of saying "we envisage a bright future," say "we see a bright future."

Instead of saying "the plan is contingent upon," say "the plan depends."

Choose short words instead of long words with the same meaning. Use layman's terms instead of jargon. Jargon is fine if you are among colleagues and people in the same profession. Otherwise, work with every day, simple English. A presentation delivered in plain simple language is easy on the ear of the listener and easy for the speaker to deliver. Comedian Jerry Seinfeld once claimed that there were times he'd spend hours trying to change an eight- word sentence to a five-word sentence while retaining its essence and humor.

Audience Sensitivity

If I were asked to state in just one sentence what this book is all about, the answer would be: It's about talking to any audience with a whole-hearted desire to please and fulfill their needs.

Many times, I have seen speakers heartlessly drone away on the subject matter of their specialty or talk charmingly and eloquently about things that are of no value to the listener. Public speaking is not about the speaker or the speaker's subject matter. Public speaking, as the words say, is for the "public."

The people dynamics behind every public speaking event can be compared to that of two lovers holding hands, walking on the beach while sharing and expressing their love for one another.

What matters most during such moments are not the things being said, but the people in the dialogue.

Keep this in mind the next time you are up on the podium. When you get up on the stage it will not be about you, your notes, or your research. It will be about the five, the fifty, or five thousand people sitting across from you. Each of those persons will be a different soul with different perspectives and life experiences.

Most speakers that we enjoy listening to are the ones who are sensitive to our needs, feelings, and wants. They talk about things that we care for and value. It is not that they do not talk about themselves – they do, but they talk about themselves in relation to the subjects which matter most to the audience. The stories they tell carry messages and benefits for the audience.

"A speech is poetry: cadence, rhythm, imagery, sweep! A speech reminds us that words, like children, have power to make dance the dullest beanbag of a heart."

- Peggy Noonan

I like to use the word "innovation" in lieu of "creativity" for a reason. I believe creativity rises from "nothingness" whereas innovation takes existing knowledge and wisdom and gives it a new twist. In public speaking innovation is adding novelty. It is being dandy and zany.

Innovation happens after you have a substantial understanding of the existing methods, ideas, and concepts about your subject.

Innovation happens when you lean back, take a larger view of existing things, and see a gap you can fill in with something different.

All throughout this book, I have been focusing on understanding and mastering the self, understanding and filling the needs of the audience, and understanding methods and techniques in preparing presentations.

You have seen existing facts and have taken an objective view of the larger picture. Now let's see if you can add a twist to what you already know and understand.

Let us review what you already know:

- Content must be valuable, precise, and relevant.
- The speech must be audience-sensitive, focused, and simple.

- Speeches and presentations must have an opening, a sequential fact-laden, fun-filled, smooth-flowing body, and a strong, dynamic closing.
- It is a good idea to set your premise, talk about your subject, and summarize or as stated before: "tell 'em what you are going to tell 'em, then tell 'em what you have to tell 'em, and then finally tell 'em what you have told 'em."

Now, what if you broke these rules a bit and tried something radical, something different, and something that will amaze the audience?

You've seen movies and plays that generally start with "Once upon a time..." and end with "...and they lived happily ever after." But there is also a genre of movies that shock you at the very beginning and keep you at the edge of your seat until the very end. Some movies make you chew your fingernails trying to figure out the ending. And there are movies that show the "meat" as an opening flashback.

You can add a twist to your speech by following some of cinema's formulas. I am talking about adding a touch of flashback, surprise, and mystery to the presentation formulas you have already learned.

To cite an example, read through the following short speech and see how I have taken a chunk from the center of the story, put it in the opening, and then delivered the head, the heart, and the humor afterwards.

THE LIGHTER SIDE OF DARKNESS

As I closed my eyes and stepped into his shoes, a chilling feeling engulfed my very soul.
The feeling of a loathsome loneliness.
The feeling of a gut-chewing, ferocious fear. And the feeling of a death-like darkness.
And yet, somehow, from within me, I found the courage to laugh just like he had done, like this: Ha! Ha! Ha!

I know! I know! I've gone ahead and you want to know who "he" is, and what am I talking about? I will tell you! But first let me tell you how I met him.

All of last year, I was depressed over several things: I was depressed because business was bad.
I was depressed because my money wasn't going far.
I was depressed because I was gaining weight and losing hair.
In fact, I was depressed about being depressed over such silly things.

One day, during this depression, I was driving home from another failed sales call. The world around me was a sad place to be in when I stopped for a traffic light on the corner of Shaw and Edsa. Pedestrians were scurrying home, cars were snarling at each other, and thirty feet above me the Light Rail Transit was hurtling away towards nowhere.

I felt sorry for the world, and I didn't feel any good about myself either.

Then, suddenly, right in the path of my car appeared a man.
His clothes were tattered, his hair was long, and his silhouette was messiah-like.
"Uh-oh!" I said to myself, "Another one of those Looney tunes!"

As he groped towards my car with an open palm, I rolled down the window hoping to get rid of him with a few coins.

Ladies and Gentlemen, on that sad, dusky evening, the face that I looked into made me jump out of my skin. Dust-covered, laden with scars, it was a face from another world.

Where his eyes should have been, there were two holes of darkness!

I gently dropped the coins into his palm, for a moment he seemed to stare at me.

He then thanked me and laughed heartily. Ha! Ha! Ha!

Laughed heartily? How could he? Was he not blind? Was he not a beggar on the streets? Where'd he get the gumption to laugh, let alone exist in this depressing world?

That is when my wandering soul abandoned me and stepped into his shoes. In his shoes I felt his loneliness, his fear, and darkness. In his shoes, I realized that the blind man was laughing in spite of his blindness.

I drove away from the corner thinking:
So what if my business was bad; at least I wasn't bankrupt! So what if my money wasn't going far; at least I wasn't broke!

So what if I was gaining weight and losing hair; I still had a great smile!
Oftentimes, we take our shortcomings and setbacks much too seriously. We dwell so much on the negative that we forget to see the humor behind things.

How many times have we lost opportunities because we thought we were not tall enough, not rich enough or not skilled enough?
How many times have we broken relationships because we thought we didn't get enough freedom, appreciation, or understanding?
Had we looked on the brighter side, we could have survived! Had we looked on the lighter side, we could have shone!

Like:
Danny de Vito who is short, bald, and ugly, and yet he is a successful actor, director, and producer.
Former Senator Juan Flavier is short, bald, comes from a humble background but he still went ahead and became the most famous Senator ever!
Comedian Marissa Sanchez constantly pokes fun at herself and becomes more and more successful.

They all started by looking at the bright side and making light of their shortcomings. Not only did they surpass their shortcomings; they outshone others.

So:
If our businesses are not making profits, think of the lighter side - turn them into non-profit organizations!
If our money is not going far, think of the lighter side - at least it's getting there faster!

If we are turning old and ugly on the outside, at least on the inside we are becoming wiser and more beautiful!
The change in our external behavior will change the way we think. The way we think and act will change our lives and our destinies!
Laugh at your failures and laugh at your foibles! Laugh if you are fat and laugh if you are thin! Laugh and your loneliness, your fears and your dejections will fizzle away!
I maintain that we may have come into this world helpless and crying; but it is within our power and capacity to go out laughing.

Laugh! Laugh! Laugh even if you have a bad accent like mine. Like this: Ha! Ha! Ha!
[Long pause]

I know! I know!
Some of you are thinking that you can out-laugh me! Right?
Sure you can! Of course you can! The power and the capacity to choose the lighter side of darkness, ladies & gentlemen, lie within you!

Chances are you are wondering where in heaven's name did Raju use a speech like that? I used it in my public-speaking gymnasium also known as the Executive Toastmasters Club of Makati. Surely, people don't speak and laugh like that in business meetings just as people don't jog, do sit-ups or stand on their heads in real life. We do all this crazy stuff to stay in shape for the real world which sometimes can be pretty weird.

But I do hope you enjoyed the rhyme, the humor and the suspense in the speech. And, I do hope it inspires you to make your real life presentations interesting and creative. It is true that the shortest route between two points is a straight line but sometimes it is fun to jump up and kick your heels in the air.

On another occasion, I was once assigned to introduce the Vice President of the Philippines Teofisto Guingona at a convention. As is usual for me, I requested a write-up on him: his educational qualifications, his achievements, and some personal information.

When I took on this speaking assignment, I did additional and lateral research - in the newspapers and the Internet. I talked to people close to him. The septuagenarian Señor Guingona was known for his oratorical speaking style and had recently been applauded for a speech he had made entitled, "I Accuse You." This was a speech he had addressed towards the then President of the Philippines, Mr. Joseph E. Estrada during his impeachment trial. The speech, rumor had it, was his best and had probably been the key to expelling the former President.

I had now found what I needed to make my introduction of the Vice President a novelty. This was my opportunity to add sparkle to an introduction which normally follows set patterns.

I ACCUSE YOU!

A little over 70 years ago in San Juan, Rizal, a little boy was born to a former senator. This boy had a wide brow, bright eyes, and a heart of gold. Like many other children of his time, he grew up in the lush, green beauty of Mindanao.

In his time, the air was pure and the water was clean; the land was filled with happiness and freedom for the Filipino.

This boy went to one of the best schools in Cagayan where he gained consistent scholastic honors. From there he moved up to Ateneo de Manila and took up Public Administration, Sociology, Economics, and Auditing.

The boy, now a man, began giving back to the world what God and life had given to him.

[illegible]

He became a teacher [illegible] Adamson University.

With every single step in life, his honesty, his hard work, and his honor took him to greater heights.

In time, he became the Governor of DBP, the President of the PCCI, a Delegate of the 1971 Constitutional Convention, the founder of SANDATA and Board Chairman of BANDILA, both socio-civic organizations.

During the Marcos era, because of his rebellion against a regime of abuses, he was jailed twice.

In a new age and during the term of President Aquino, he became the Chairman of the Commission on Audit, earned a reputation as a no- nonsense administrator, and was invited to be a Senator.

Later in the Senate, he was appointed President Pro-Tempore. He also served as chairman of the Blue Ribbon Committee.

He filed several bills that would form and shape a newly recovered democracy.

His provincial kababayans appointed him as director and chairman of the Mindanao Development Authority.

During the term of President Fidel Ramos, he was the Executive Secretary and the Justice Secretary.

He approached and handled both jobs with flair and untarnished fairness.

During the following years, this man, who was turning into a greater human being, became a graft buster. He jailed rapists, arrested murderers, and put away dangerous drug dealers.
Last year, amidst a national crisis, this larger-than-life human being stood up alone and was instrumental in toppling another unwanted regime with a speech entitled, "I Accuse You." He thereby created and brought about new change for the country of his love, the Philippines.

Now you might think that all this person did was do justice, bring about peace, and churn development and growth, thereby acquiring laurels and accolades for himself. No, that is not true.

There was a time when this man with a golden heart also chased, wooed, and romanced a beautiful mestiza by the name of Ruthie de Lara. He nicknamed her "Ting" and won her heart and hand in marriage. Today, he has three good-looking and successful protégés and replicas of himself with Ruthie.

A newly formed government and the people of the Philippines recognized and respected the worth and value of this Son of Mindanao and made him the Vice President of the Philippines.
In this post, he still dreams and works for a country of his childhood, a country with clean air, pure water, happiness, and freedom for his fellow Filipinos.

Today, he is amongst us to share his dreams and work with us because his dream is also the dream of us Fil-Indians.

I repeat:
"His dream is also the dream of us Fil-Indians"
His dream of a country with pure water, clean air, happiness, growth and development for every human that lives and breathes on this land.

Ladies and Gentlemen, with the permission of our chief guest, I humbly...

I accuse him of being a lover of life, a husband, and a father. I accuse him of being a teacher, a lawyer, and a legislator.
I accuse him of being a senator, a book writer, and a statesman par excellence!

Ladies and Gentlemen: I take special pride and honor in presenting to you a man with a heart of gold, a true blue Son of Mindanao, and above all, a Filipino and the Vice President of the Republic of the Philippines: Señor Teofisto T. Guingona, Jr.

Notice the repetition, rhyme and humor that are situational and inoffensive. The introduction left the audience smiling from ear to ear and our chief guest thrilled to the bone.

To prepare a good speech you must take the shortest route from point to point, but sometimes it is nice to jump up in the air and kick your heels on the way.

The chairman of Sony Corp. has rightly said this about being innovative:

> *"Let us not give the customer what he can imagine,*
> *Let us give him what he has never imagined!"*

Writing for the Eyes, Ears, and Body

The learning styles of adults as we discussed in Chapter 2 are:

- Visual
- Auditory
- Kinesthetic

When writing your speech, remember to appeal to your listener's ways of absorbing information. Give them something that they can almost see, hear, or touch. As you finish your speech drafts and are at your second or third rewrite, it is time to check if you have created enough word pictures for your "Visual" audience – words that conjure up images that are colorful and real enough to be touched.

For example:

The window by my bed is as big as the wall itself and looks out towards the eastern sky through patches of green sycamore.

On mornings when I wake up, I hear the birds chirp as the sunshine slowly seeps through the leaves and onto the black-brown hair of my wife beside me. She looks gentle, sweet, and very vulnerable as she lies bundled amongst the sheets.

These words not only create a picture, but also add reality to the "Visuals." These easy, colorful words put a smile on the listener's face.

Not all presentations, however, allow us the liberty of getting picturesque with our words; some have to cater to the needs of the Auditory Learner and be quite literal. In cases like these, a clear-cut, logical listing of ideas would enhance the clarity of your presentation.

For Example:

The first thing that we need to do to reduce our air conditioning costs is to insulate the roof.

The second thing is to close all air leaks and exits followed by maintaining cleanliness and housekeeping policies that prevent litter, dust, and the use of smoke-emitting appliances.

The Kinesthetic, on the other hand, requires that we stimulate their sense of smell, touch, and feeling. Here we can use words that are descriptive and vivid.

For Example:

"As his coarse and grubby hands landed on my bare chest and pushed me hard, I stumbled backward in a state of shock and landed on the gravel, wounding my elbows and hands. A mad rage went through me as I grabbed the cold, angular rock from the ground and lunged towards him with a silent scream in my lungs."

Using your imagination, working with words, and moving from one learning style to another will keep your talk interesting and entertain all types of audiences.

On the next page is an illustration of what should be happening with all the pre-work you are doing before finalizing a speech. The four stages are comparable to the first, the second and the third layer to the Heart of Public Speaking.

Stages before writing a speech

Research Stage

- Do a self-analysis.
- Analyze audience needs and objectives.
- Go through all possible resources. Gather information.
- Reject very little data. Mind Map® several inputs.
- Do not write down anything yet. Writing will bind you down to the written word. Let several ideas and possibilities "percolate" in your mind.

Planning Stage

- Plan on resources you will use.
- Your mind is already picking and choosing the best, deliverable ideas and information is taking shape.
- Reject some information; share ideas with others
- Start keeping and making notes.

Preparing Stage

- Decide on format, structures, themes, hooks, and style.
- Reject some more data. Mind Map® flow and content.
- Start writing a large, first draft.
- Take options on clarity, creativity, and language.
- Do several edits and assess flow of thoughts

Deliverable Speech

- Cut down all frill. Make the speech time-bound.
- Maintain persuasiveness and impact.
- Ensure smoothness and simplicity to make your points easier to remember.
- Mind Map® to be able to deliver conversationally.

SPEAK IT OUT
DRAFT IT
WRITE & REWRITE AGAIN
HEAR IT BACK OFTEN
TRASH A LOT.
LESS IS MORE
FINAL
FINAL PRESENTATION

Creating Visual Aids for all Learning Styles

Visual aids can be fun or they can be boring. They should be fun, suggestive, and interesting. Gone are the days when you had to use a blackboard, flipcharts, etc. Today, technology is so advanced and intuitive that it would be a sin not to make the most of it. I am not saying that the visuals should outshine our presentation, but rather like an interesting ensemble behind it, just like the background music score of a good movie scene enhances the action and the dialogue. Our visuals must be the backdrop— subtle, suggestive, and sequential. Visuals must carry images and colors that fit into the speaker's topic.

A year ago, I was into the third day of a workshop titled "Power Speaking Skills Through Mind Mapping®." Throughout I had emphasized to the participants the importance of audience needs, sensitivity, connectivity, dialogue, rapport, communication, awareness, need for humor, and the supportive role of visual aids. That afternoon, all of the participants had prepared sample presentations, and many of them were without visual aids.

Then one of the senior participants, a businessman, [illegible] [illegible] Power Point presentation that had music and other special effec[illegible] He spoke clearly, with a confident voice and his words resonated with the pictures and the effects on the screen behind him. Not for one moment did he lose the rhythm or the attention of his audience.

Some participants later questioned my earlier insistence of the speaker being the main presentation himself. I explained that as long as we did not feel overwhelmed and as long as we felt the personal connection and understood the talk well, then the balance between an "organic" and a "technical" presentation was well achieved.

Here are nine tips on how to prepare great visuals:

- Put text on a background that is not too colorful or distracting.

- Wherever possible, put in images instead of words and numbers.
- Make sentences short and precise.
- Follow the 3 x 5 rule in your visuals
  a. a maximum of 3 lines in a large font
  b. a maximum of 5 words to a single line.
- Keep moving objects, images, and special effects to a minimum.
- The timing of the effects should be synchronized with your speaking.
- Expose information and details slowly. One idea or a sentence at a time.
- When using overhead transparencies, cover part of the information with a blank sheet of paper and slide it down slowly from one sentence to the next. This is called the "striptease" method.
- Follow the same design, theme, font, and color for all slides.
- Number your slides/transparencies to allow you to move back and forth with ease.

Throughout a visual presentation, make sure that you do not become hooked and dependent on the visuals. Don't end up just reading them! Your visuals have to present something that supports what you are saying or "rephrase" in images the speech that you are delivering in words. Your visuals are not your speech, they must stay an aid and not become a crutch.

Speeches that "Have to be Read!"

I am a devout proponent of speaking without notes, but there are times when speeches need to be read out to an audience. These could be very technical presentations or very formal ones. Here are eight easy tips that will help you read as if you were speaking conversationally.

These tips are a synthesis between a well-written linear text and an organic, free flowing Mind Map®.

Before you follow the eight easy steps, please make sure:

- The content is relevant, valuable, and precise.
- The presentation has a strong opening and a closing.
- The middle is filled with sufficient supporting facts and figures, wherever necessary.
- The content is sprinkled with humor and has anecdotes that add flavor to the facts.
- To do a final "word count" to gauge approximate time.
- To do a spell and grammar check.
- To read out loud your written material to a colleague to test the flow of ideas.
- To change the language wherever possible to sound like the spoken word.

Now, here is how to lay out written material so that reading it becomes easy and effective:

- Maintain a large left margin and keep the bulk of the text towards the right.
- Use the large left margin for prompts and cues for dramatic pauses, smiles and other gestures.
- Use several colors in the main text to show variation in pausing, pacing or pitch. If you are building up a tempo from annoyance to rage, go from yellow, to orange, to red in text color.
- Leave a large lower margin. This allows you to slide one page over another thereby letting you read more smoothly. Flipping pages breaks the rhythm and hampers connectivity with your audience.
- Also add images or little icons wherever you can't express in words your cues or prompts. Images are a relief and let you get creative with your delivery.
- Keep the font size of the main text as large as possible. This makes easy reading and prevents squinting or

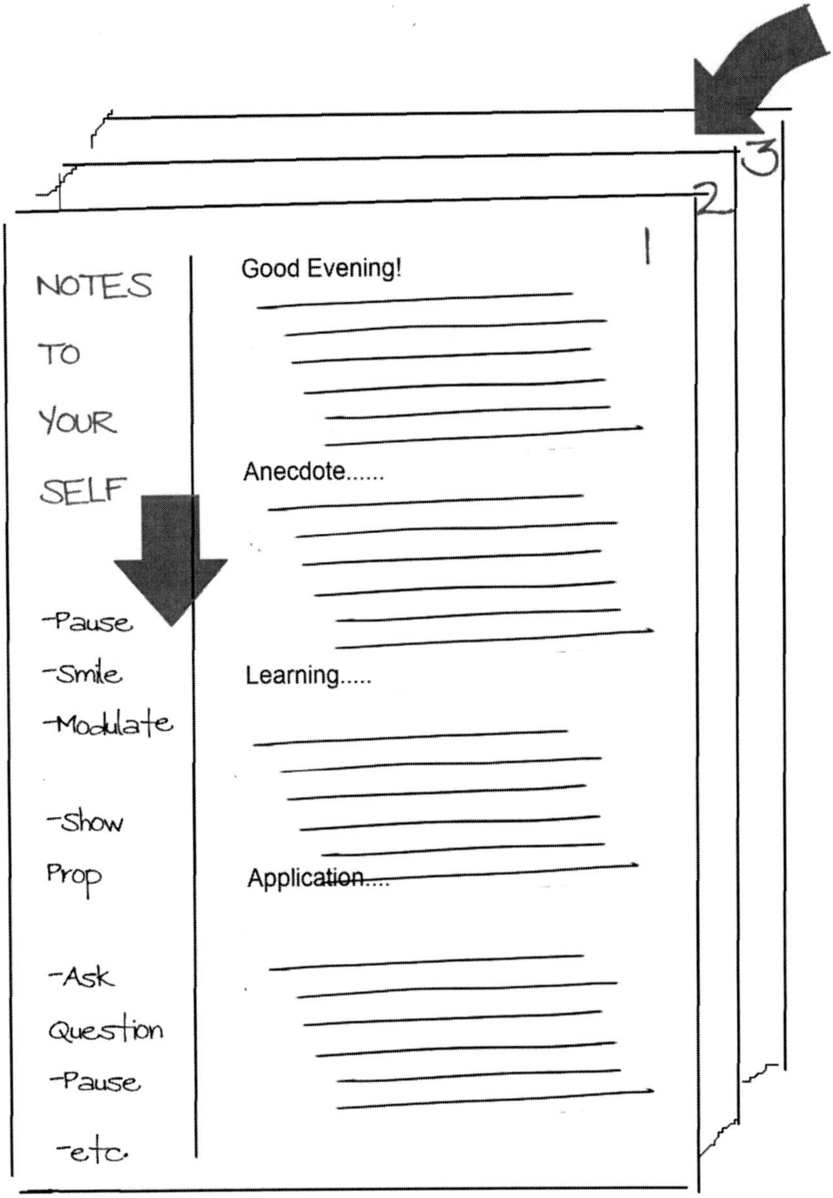

HOW TO READ A SPEECH

- Fumbling with reading glasses. I have found font size 20 very readable from a standing position on a lectern.
- Underline certain key words that may have been your links to additional information from your Mind Mapping® exercise. In case you need to expound further and break away from "reading," these key words will stimulate thought.
- Finally, please do number all the pages. I have heard stories about speech sheets getting mixed up and the speaker spending embarrassing moments trying to sort them out and talk at the same time. Once, a Japanese diplomat was given by his secretary two non-collated, non-numbered copies of one speech as a precaution, and he ended up reading each page of his presentation twice!

3.0 Insights on Writing a Speech

3.1 Write your material and maintain the volume of content based on the allotted time.

3.2 It is always polite to start on time and finish off a few minutes before you are supposed to.

3.3 Keep your message and content focused towards the objective; do not deviate.

3.4 Keep your language simple, straight, and your ideas sequential.

3.5 A proper sequence can be broken to add surprise, mystery, and to increase the interest of the audience.

3.6 Wherever possible add dialogue and word pictures to your speeches.

3.7 When reading speeches, read from big print and maintain eye contact with your audience.

3.0 Exercises

3.1. Read out loud any two pages from the book and record your reading time.

Read out loud to a group of people and record the time. Record your own voice while reading (using a voice recorder) after re-writing or editing parts of it.

Average all the above time records to get a more accurate record of your speaking rate per minute.

3.2 Using your speaking rate in words per minute as derived from the above exercise, prepare a 10 minute persuasive presentation to a friend on the "Benefits of Giving Up Smoking."

3.3 Using the same presentation, type it on a computer as described in 3.6 with delivery cues and pause notations to yourself and then read it out loud to a group of people. Use gestures and modulate your voice often.

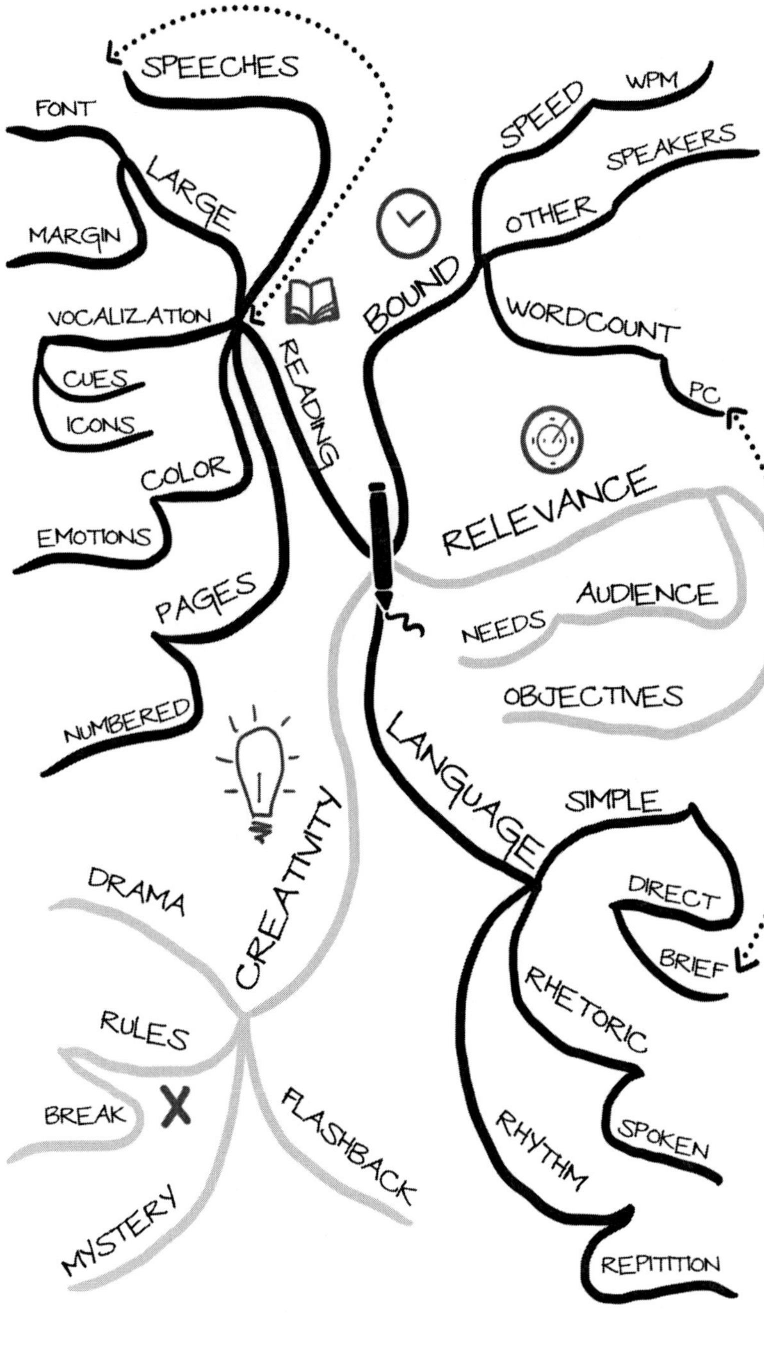

A Mind Map on Writing

Chapter Four
How to Prepare for Speaking

Remember that fear always lurks behind perfectionist. Confronting your fears and allowing yourself the right to be human can, paradoxically, make you a far happier and more productive person.

- Dr. David M. Burns

Life Layers: Understanding Authenticity

Deep within the layers of your brain lies the amygdala –what is also referred to as the "reptilian brain." This is the part of the brain that exercises no logic, rationality, or order. It is the part of the brain that thrives on passion, fear, and rage. It is the reactive brain.

In the amygdala lie emotions that are unclear at times and emotions that are very difficult to manage. Fear of things, real or imagined, is one of these emotions. This is the same fear that can make or break you as a human being and also as a public speaker.

The "fight or flight" syndrome is an element of this fear that resides in your innermost brain. Manifestations of this syndrome range from not wanting to stand up and speak at all or avoiding the spotlight altogether. Also sweaty palms and brows, increased heartbeat, a parched throat, and knocking knees are all manifestations of the same fear.

A veteran speaker friend of mine, Gina Mapua, once told me about a public speaking school in Australia where they have a waist-high corral to prevent speakers from walking away until they have finished speaking. She also recounts a story of how a six-foot tall man, literally toppled over the corral from fear of speaking to a group.

I do not know how much truth there is to the story, but I've had occasions when I have personally stumbled while getting up on the podium, sometimes fumbling for a long time with the mike to overcome my nervousness. Nervousness and fear are universal. People like Abraham Lincoln, Winston Churchill, Laurence Olivier, and even Ronald Reagan have confessed to fighting constant battles with these two emotions.

The roots of these fears lie in our prehistoric origins. Man as a hunter and prey had to be on guard for predators and fierce creatures. As one among many creatures that roamed the world, he couldn't afford to be taken by surprise. He had to be constantly vigilant against things he couldn't see or understand, and things that appeared in his own imagination.

Today, modern man may not have to be on constant guard against bloodthirsty predators, but corporate life and massive amounts of interpersonal exchanges can cause harm to one's psyche and confidence. In such moments, this ancient malady still rises from your depths and wreaks havoc on your external behavior.

The brain's outer cortex, the cerebellum, is the rational, cognizant part of the brain. The cerebellum may make all the preparations, do research, and put in a lot of practice, but until the inner mind is not soothed, calmed, and relaxed, the outer performance will be jerky, dissonant, and sloppy. Self-doubt, low confidence, and lack of self-esteem stem from deep-seated fears. Fighting these internal demons is and will always be a lifelong battle.

As a defense mechanism, you try to cover up this fear. You pretend not to have it. You try to hide it by speaking in a loud, false voice or through excessive interaction with the audience or co-speakers.

Once, I observed a sales director of a large multi-level marketing company who had the habit of calling for a round of applause every few minutes during his speech. In the din of the applause, he'd gulp in air to soothe his fears and then continue, until it was time to call for another round of applause.

Other speakers I've seen speak loudly above the heads of their audience, or speak fast and furiously, hoping to finish off the "fight" before their legs give in to "flight."

Behind the fear, behind the façade of confidence and the loud, speaking voice lie these demons. To excel as public speakers, you need to constantly reach in and reclaim your strong inner being. This inner being is the source of reality and authenticity. It is the cool confidence that surfaces every time we reach in and speak from there. Within this authentic inside lies the heart of public speaking that helps bring about a renaissance of thoughts and action.

Authenticity is achieved by an honest appraisal of your objectives, purpose, and ulterior motives.

The person who speaks from the heart speaks plainly, directly, and with undeniable honesty. No matter how bad the structure, the format, or the language of his speech, it becomes what my teenage kids call "real!"

Many years ago, Mario Garrolini, a speaker friend of mine died in a motorcycle accident. He was Italian and his job involved conducting technical workshops for a large manufacturing company. Several of his friends from the speaking and training business turned up to give eulogies at his wake.

Several of them spoke about his past, his character, and their relationship with him.

They all spoke with eloquence, wit and style but the speaker that stood out and outshone them all was an old, humble, Filipino mechanic.

He came up with stooped shoulders, wrung his hands in agony, and stumbled through every word he was uttering while clutching the front of his shirt tightly. He spoke of how much he loved Mario and shared happy little anecdotes of their friendship.

His language was simple, he wasn't stylish or educated, but as he spoke, there were tears and laughter in his eyes. After he finished there were tears and laughter in the eyes of everyone present. He was speaking the plain truth in simple words.

There are times when I get anxious and obsessed with my own importance before speaking. But the moment I remember that old, humble, Filipino mechanic and the authenticity of his words, I become "real."

Let's examine the layers between our behavior and our inner source of authenticity:

- The layer of pretension. The most external layer wherein we pretend to be important, powerful, and far too different from the person we really are.
- The layer of fear. Also an external layer that we create when we try to please others or are afraid of the consequences of being ourselves.
- The innermost layer of authenticity. Herein we are peaceful, happy and completely honest about ourselves.

Tap into the innermost layer before preparing a speech, and your speech will shine and surprise even you.

Building Confidence through Vulnerability

I have found that being honest about what you know and don't know levels out any misconceptions that the audience might have of you during and after the speech. I am a non-believer in the adage of "fake it until you make it." I'd rather be honest, work hard and straight, and then "make it" so I don't have to "fake it."

Living this principle makes you strong and pure inside. There are times that when you do confess ignorance, you become vulnerable. But being vulnerable makes you endearing and human. People relate to vulnerability much more than they can understand and accept pretension or behavior that rises out of fear.

One day, Distinguished Toastmaster Herbert Lee, a speaker/ trainer friend of mine, spoke about how important it is to expose your inner self to create a better rapport. "You gotta open your hearts!" he cried. To prove this point to his audience he unbuttoned the front of his jacket, yanked his necktie off, and grabbed his shirt by the collar as if to rip it off. The audience leaned back and gasped, not knowing what was coming next. With a flourish, my friend tore the shirt off his body, leaving his jacket on. The audience erupted into amazed laughter when they realized his shirt was a trick-shirt designed to be ripped off and away from under his jacket!

Inner Work: Overcoming Anxiety and Fear

You gain strength, courage and confidence
by every experience in which you really stop
to look fear in the face. You are able to say
to yourself. "I have lived through this horror.
I can take the next thing that comes along."
You must do the thing you think you cannot do.

- Eleanor Roosevelt

THE LITTLE FELLOW ON YOUR SHOULDER

Generally speaking there are three entities in a conference hall. One is your audience, who is there to receive the gift of your knowledge and convictions. Second is you, the speaker, who, as a speaker, are there to share your knowledge and convictions.

And then there is that "little fellow on your shoulder."

When you prepare to speak, you have a critical alter ego that nags you about your ineptness and lists all the things that can go wrong when you get up to speak. Then there is also another alter ego that supports, encourages, and inspires you. This ego will tell you all positive things that you can do and achieve as a speaker and as a person.

I like calling these two contrasting elements "that little fellow on your shoulder." This little fellow can sit on your shoulder and scare you into failure and depression. It is the same little fellow that can also inspire, motivate, and make you reach for higher objectives.

The idea is to become aware of this fellow. Recognize him as someone you cannot do away with but you can consciously will him to support, encourage, and inspire you. I practice this trick all the time. The moment I recognize the dual nature of this little fellow on my shoulder a smile comes to my face and it becomes a cinch to move into a positive, driven, calm attitude. It works for me and I promise you it will work for you!

Recognizing the elements of your fear will help you overcome them. You have learned that reality, sincerity, and authenticity are major factors that can help you overcome your fears. While preparing to deliver a speech, ask yourself the following questions. Honest answers to these questions will ease your anxiety and establish your real goals.

Is the content of my speech true?

- *If there are facts, numbers or anecdotes that you are not sure of, not using them will cut down your anxiety.*

Am I telling half-truths and avoiding facts?

- *If you are vague about concepts and are avoiding the real issues just so that you can fulfill the task of presenting, then you will be doubtful and fearful.*

Will the content of my speech do some other person or entity undue harm?

- *If ever you have a hidden agenda of discrediting someone else there is a good possibility that the audience will see through you and be non-responsive and hostile towards you.*

What is my ulterior motive for saying certain things in my speech?

- *If your motives are well meaning and will truly benefit the audience, it becomes easier to speak with power, style and confidence.*

There are other methods of managing and overcoming anxiety and fear and these are discussed in Chapter 5: Practicing a Speech.

Believing in the Message you Deliver

In the latter part of his life, Mahatma Gandhi was once asked what the message of his life was and he replied, "My life is my message."

Gandhi believed in the innate goodness of humankind and his means of reclaiming that innate goodness was assertiveness through non-violence. That was essentially his message, his life. With that message, he was able to unite several hundreds of state- kingdoms, cultures, and communities. With that message he was able to set India free from the English, giving birth to a nation which today is the world's largest democracy.

Gandhi spoke, inspired, and rallied millions of people towards one goal through just one message. He had no doubts, no ulterior motive, and therefore no fear. He did not want to become King, President or the biggest shareholder of an enterprise called India.

Likewise, whether we are marketing heads or organizational leaders, we can create value and purpose in the little things we do and thereby bring about positive change.

The quality and the effectiveness of your speeches will match the quality and effectiveness of your message.

If you have thus far, while preparing your presentation, gone through the stages then from now on tapping into your authentic nature and expressing truths, overcoming anxiety through deep introspection will consistently help you easily connect, engage and influence others. This process is the ultimate Heart of Public Speaking.

4.0 Insights on Preparing for a Speech

4.1 Soothe and calm the inner mind before doing physical movements to overcome your fear.

4.2 As long as there is authenticity in your message and your objectives are real, overcoming jitters will become easier.

4.3 Verify the objectives of the message from the point of view of the audience rather than your own.

4.4 Examine your own character well and present yourself as who you really are. Increasing your self-confidence will then become a cinch.

4.5 Let your inner critic be kind and gentle.

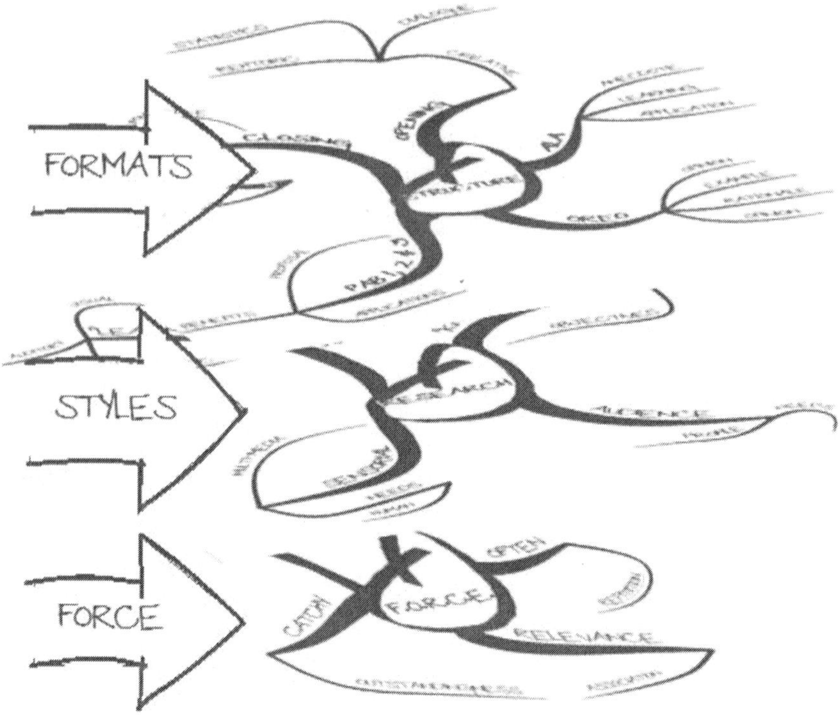

The three heart principles stacked together will serve as working template for you to plan, prepare, write, practice and deliver speeches that will be powerful and consistently effective.

4.0 Exercises

1. The three "Life Layers" in most people are:
   - The outer layer of P _ _ _ _ _ _ _ _ _
   - The middle layer of F _ _ _
   - The inner most layer of A _ _ _ _ _ _ _ _ _ _ _

2. Relate a story of a personal experience that created a deep impact on your beliefs and personality.

   ____

   ____

   ____

   ____

3. Write down at least three things that you are afraid of during public speaking and explain why.

   ____

   ____

   ____

   ____

4. If you did not have these fears, how would you see yourself performing and handling occasions of public speaking?

   ____

   ____

   ____

   ____

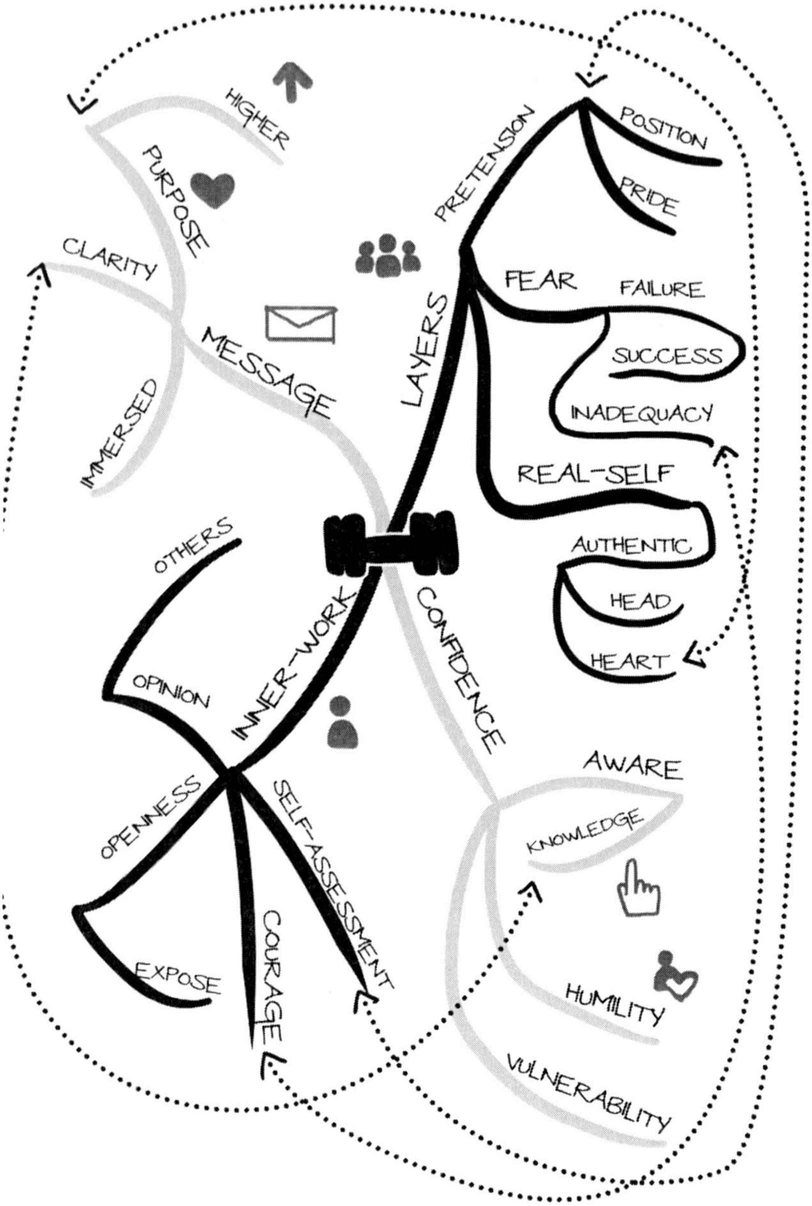

A Mind Map on Preparing for a Speech

Chapter Five
How to Practice a Speech

What a talker he is! But lately he's developed a slight impediment in his speech. He stops to breathe!

- Fred Metcalf

The Life in Breathing

Several years ago, I was to do the welcome remarks at a business gathering for an audience of over 500 people. Even though I had prepared and practiced my speech, I was very nervous. One of my colleagues, Adrian Martinez, a trainer by profession and a philosopher by nature, was in the audience. I walked up to him and expressed my anxiety and nervousness.

> *"Breathe," he said to me softly. I started taking in gulps of air, inhaling and exhaling. "No, not now. Breathe during the speech!" he said.*
>
> *"You mean while I am up there, talking?"*
>
> *"Yeah! Relax now and breathe while you are speaking," he said.*

As I walked up to the microphone, I met Adrian's eyes in the audience and remembered the suggestion. When I began speaking I maintained a mindful awareness on my breathing. I breathed in calmly like a baby throughout my talk. I ended up delivering my speech in the most relaxed and confident manner and with my best voice ever! All I did was stay relaxed and aware of my breathing.

The word anxiety comes from the Latin word "angere," which means to choke. When we are anxious, our psyche literally puts a stranglehold on our breathing. Breathing consciously and deliberately releases us from that grip of anxiety. Once we are free, all our systems and senses work in resonance.

The richness of our voice permeates through our vocal chords through breathing. Our eyesight, our facial expressions, and our body movements are fresh, healthy, and wholesome. Breathing in and out from the depths of our lungs elates our mood and helps awaken our inner being, which naturally goads us into seeking higher purposes and higher objectives in whatever we do.

Take note of moments and times in your life when you have been completely at ease with yourself and with your surroundings. Such moments happen to us when we are around nature, on the mountains or by the beach. These are also the moments where we are breathing well.

Breathing well is achieved by becoming conscious of it, by constantly trying to improve the quality of our breathing. Here is an exercise that I recommend you practice every day. Repeat it several times on the day you are to speak, and moments before you are going to speak.

First, take note of your body position. Do you feel as if you are sitting uncomfortably or standing with tension in your legs, torso, or shoulder? Find the tension wherever it exists in your body. Imagine releasing that tension into the air.

Second, get extremely comfortable. If you are sitting on a chair, lean against it and let the chair support all your weight. If you are standing, spread your feet to shoulder width, and press down on them. Visualize your body hanging loosely on a very straight frame. Do not tighten your jaws or shoulder blades.

Once you are in a straight and steady position, bring your attention to your breathing. Visualize the pure air going through your right nostril, flowing into your bronchial tubes, and spreading into your lungs. Then imagine your diaphragm rise up to expand the lungs as they take in more air and spread it among the alveoli in your lungs. Imagine your alveoli use the oxygen to purify your blood, take out the impurities, and pump them out through the bronchial tubes and out of your left nostril.

Do this at an even pace. Do it consciously but without getting too anxious about it. If your mind strays away, bring back your attention to the exercise and very soon you will notice your anxiety and tension wearing off.

You may do this exercise not just for public speaking but also to alleviate your stress from everyday life.

Your Voice: The Punch behind your Personality

If the eyes are the windows to your soul then your voice is the music that bursts from your soul. Your voice is a "proxy" of your personality that doesn't require your physical presence. It tells as much about your personality as your eyes tell about your soul.

The quality of your voice, just like the color of your eyes, is God-given. But the personality of your voice is what you make of it by way of inflection, enunciation, and vocalization. Deep, baritone, rich voices can sometimes sound harsh, flat, and dissonant while low, soft, thin voices can, with proper modulation, be pleasant to the ear.

Your voice is the product of air passing through your vocal chords, mouth, and lips. You may not have much of a say as to what kind of vocal chords you get in life, but you can surely play sweet music with the air that strums your vocal chords and escapes through your mouth, tongue, and lips. The personality of your voice is then largely dependent on how you manage your breathing.

I admire the way former U.S. President Bill Clinton, Indian Superstar Amitabh Bachchan, and Asian MTV Host Donita Rose modulate their voices. Each of them has a different voice quality and accent but all three of them understand timing, rhythm, and inflection. It is also very obvious from the way they speak that they have a high awareness of their talent. They like what they can do with their voices and they use it for maximum effect.

At a workshop some time ago, one of my participants related a story about how he had seen Amitabh Bachchan prepare himself for a scene which required him to get into a rage and still deliver his lines with clarity, rhythm, and perfect enunciation.

Away from the set and the cameras, in a corner, Mr. Bachchan was, seemingly, screaming and shouting at the wall. My participant went up and asked Mr. Bachchan the reason behind this strange behavior. The legendary star replied that he was not only preparing his physiology to emote anger, but also exercising his vocal chords and diaphragm to deliver with power and clarity the lines for the next scene.

The mastery of rhythm and timing that many good public speakers have is achieved through hours of practice and discipline. We too can improve our vocal delivery through exercise and discipline.

Let's start off by assessing the personality of your voice. Take a quality tape recorder and read something out loud for 10 minutes.

- Were you rushing through the words?
- Were you in a hurry to get it over with?
- While recording, were you breathing normally?
- Because you were recording, were you trying to sound professional?
- Were you trying to imitate someone else's speaking style?
- Were you pronouncing the vowels from the depths of your diaphragm?
- Were you enunciating the consonants completely and carefully?

Do several tests on yourself. You will find there will be a voice that sounds rich, distinct and conversational. That is the voice you need to capture and train for public speaking.

When I first started in public speaking, I spoke in a voice that truly reflected my personality. But after a few months of training, my trainers made me conscious of several superfluous things like my Fil-Indian accent or the way I pronounced certain words.

Fear and anxiety replaced my natural personality until I realized that I was hurting myself trying to sound like someone else. Today, I have found my voice and people comment positively on not only what I say, but also on the way I say it.

Here are several ways to enhance the personality of your voice:

- Stand erect and let the air from the depths of your diaphragm rise to modulate your voice.
- Speak deliberately and raise the volume to a level, which is slightly above your conversational voice.
- Speak in a large room as if you were speaking to the person farthest away from you.
- Pause every so often and run the next few sentences through your mind before you speak. Don't worry. The brain thinks in images. You will be able to visualize your sentences and modulate better in the slight pauses that you allow yourself.
- Don't abuse your vocal chords by smoking or drinking caffeine that dehydrates your mouth and tongue. Drink warm water instead of coffee before a speech.
- When using a sound system, test it first. And while speaking, stay at a proper distance from the microphone so that it does not cause vibrations or echoes.
- Lastly, breathe easily and steadily while speaking.

Learn to listen to yourself more often. Listen to your own speeches and watch videos of yourself whenever possible. Constantly work at improving vocalization and adding rhythm and timing to the way you speak.

The Power of the Pause

Across the world, hundreds of times, I have seen speakers fail to use sufficient and well-timed pauses in their delivery and thus mess up what could have been awe-inspiring performances. A pause is a break in the established flow of words in a speech. It allows for time needed in absorbing ideas that have already been expressed.
A pause allows both speaker and listeners to gather their thoughts and get ready for the oncoming ideas and suggestions. Pauses, when used properly with rhythm, improve the whole quality of a speech. International motivational speaker Zig Ziglar uses pauses with such melody that listening to him becomes a soothing and magical experience. A proper pause placed well between ideas and examples helps the audience understand and digest ideas better. A pause rightly timed, and managed well, magnifies the beauty hidden in the words of a speech. It enhances and illuminates the wisdom that is shared in quality conversations and presentations.

In the movie Karate Kid there is a scene where Mr. Miyagi, the Japanese karate master, is trimming a bonsai tree and Daniel, the Karate Kid, comes up to him inquiring:

> *Daniel: "Hey, Mr. Miyagi, what're you doing?"*
>
> *Mr. Miyagi: "I am creating space."*
>
> *Daniel: "You are trimming the leaves and the branches."*
>
> *Mr., Miyagi: "No. I am beautifying the space between."*
>
> *Daniel: "You kidding me, Mr. Miyagi?"*
>
> *Mr. Miyagi: "You see, Danielsan, Bonsai is not the art of beautifying the tree and the leaves. It is the art of beautifying the space between the leaves and the branches."*

There is much Zen wisdom in the above dialogue that can be compared to the importance of pausing between the flow of words. Pausing with style and rhythm for effect has a fantastic impact on the audience and makes your speech just as compellingly beautiful as a bonsai tree.

I am also partial to a planned pause at the beginning, before starting up to speak. This is also a pause that most speakers sometimes forget to employ. It is a pause that must be practiced by all budding and experienced speakers. This pause, as you stand up to speak, must be quiet, and prayerful and must allow the audience to make silent, visual contact with you. This silent moment becomes the cornerstone of great conversation that follows, because silence is the beginning of all dialogue. In this moment, when we stand up to speak, we can smile at the audience, let them accept us as we are, while we gather our thoughts and prepare to project what lies in our minds and hearts. This is the calm, which must be deliberately practiced, before generating the storm of all creative and fruitful dialogue.

Similarly, a pause at the end of a presentation while smiling at the audience signifies gratitude and affiliation with the audience.

Practice finishing your speech and then standing still for a few seconds while letting the audience accept closure and completion of the interaction. This last silent moment is a powerful way of saying "thank you" without using any words.

Body Language and Facial Expressions

Have you ever been in a room full of people when a well-groomed, tall, dark, and handsome man walks in? All eyes turn towards him and people start listing down positive assumptions about him. If in the same room an old, simply dressed woman walks in people give her little attention. There are no guarantees as to which of them is a better speaker, but people are generally receptive and open to appearances.

Likewise, when you take the first few steps towards the lectern people take note of your posture, stride, and the way you meet their eyes. These are actually manifestations of your personality, mood, and level of confidence. If you walk with stooped shoulders, you create a gloomy impression which will influence the mood in the room. On the other hand, if you walk up with confident strides and head held high, you create a positive sense of expectation and excitement in the audience.

> *Research says that 58% of impact and effect of a presentation is made up by body language, 35% by voice projection and facial expression, while only 7% by the words and content.*

This means that even if your content is well written but delivered in a sloppy and dull manner, your presentation will not bring about the desired effect, while a presentation that lacks information but is delivered with enthusiasm and a lot of conviction will have a better and lasting effect on the listeners.

Since body language and gestures represent so much of what goes on inside you, the real work needs to be done on the inside rather than just the outside. Doing a substantial amount of inner work also helps us maintain healthy eye contact and high audience engagement. On the other hand, if you are not comfortable with yourself, your topic, and your audience, the agitated look on your face will be hard to hide.

Therefore, take steps first to:

- Know yourself very well. Understand your motives and purpose.
- Maintain a larger, happier view of things.
- Deeply and thoroughly research, study, prepare, plan, and practice your material
- Have the audience's needs and importance at the top of your mind.
- Be authentic, purposeful, and honest.

The other external things that you can to do to improve your body language are:

- Stay fit and healthy with a regular exercise routine.
- Dress well and pay attention to your grooming.
- Stride into the room and to the lectern as if with a happy purpose. People will take note of this.
- Before you start speaking, stand in the center of the stage or behind the lectern. As you stand, plant your feet firmly on the ground, visualize your body as erect and stretching upwards from the crown of your head.
- Keep a straight, level head towards your audience or the camera.
- Take a bigger picture of the surroundings and manage your materials and visual aids.
- Do not fumble with yourself, your clothes, pencil, paper, etc.,
- Start speaking slowly and calmly while breathing evenly from the depths of your diaphragm.
- Keep your hands loose by your sides or hold them in front of your belly, relaxed fingers touching as if you were praying.

- Don't plan on any mechanical movements because your hands will naturally follow your words and your passion for the subject.
- Be cool, calm, collected, and as rational as possible. Your message and your beliefs will carry you well.
- While delivering your presentation, stay elated and energetic and your audience will be able to gauge your confidence when watching you.

Your enthusiasm, passion, and knowledge of the topic will be seen and heard by your audience. One valuable feature that you can add to your presence is a smile. When you smile you are telling the audience that you like them, you like what you're telling them, and that you have self-confidence. A smile engages the audience and encourages them to listen to what you have to say. To top this, a genuine smile from the heart reaches your eyes easily, making them light up. The idea is to get as expressive as possible but not become mechanical and forced. Apply the lessons from the learning styles as studied in Chapter 1. Maximize multi-sensorial transfer using positive and graceful gestures.

So, before it is time for you to face your audience, walk up to a mirror and size yourself up. At the mirror seek authenticity before appearance, willingness to give value before applause, calm confidence before concerns, fear and agitation. Should there be any negative emotions, get rid of them through positive questioning in the light of what you want to give rather than what you want to get from the audience. Place the needs and the desires of the audience before your own and slowly but surely your mood will change. You will acquire an air of courage and peace which will appear on your face and in your posture. Now take a few deep breathes, shake your limbs, do some loud humming to warm up your vocal chords and then boldly and purposefully walk up to the stage. Your audience will notice the brilliance that radiates from you at first glance. They will be pleased with and receptive to the confidence your stride and squared shoulders exude. Their enhanced sense of acceptance and happiness will inspire you to perform whole-heartedly. Remember, the road to creative excellence is a two-way street and is filled with support and good vibes between speaker and audience.

Facial Expressions

If a man insisted always on being Serious, and never allowed himself a bit of fun and relaxation, he would go mad or become Unstable without knowing it.

- Heredotus

Your enthusiasm, passion, and knowledge of the topic will be seen and heard by your audience. One valuable feature that you can add to your presence is a smile.

When you smile you are telling the audience that you like them, you like what you're telling them, and that you have self-confidence. A smile engages the audience and encourages them to listen to what you have to say. To top this, a genuine smile from the heart reaches your eyes easily, making them light up.

The idea is to get as expressive as possible but not become mechanical and forced. Apply the lessons from the learning styles as studied in Chapter 1. Maximize multi-sensorial transfer using positive and graceful gestures.

So, before it is time for you to face your audience, walk up to a mirror and size yourself up. At the mirror seek authenticity before appearance, willingness to give value before applause, calm confidence before concerns, fear and agitation. Should there be any negative emotions, get rid of them through positive questioning in the light of what you want to give rather than what you want to get from the audience. Place the needs and the desires of the audience before your own and slowly but surely your mood will change. You will acquire an air of courage and peace which will appear on your face and in your posture. Now take a few deep breathes, shake your limbs, do some loud humming to warm up your vocal chords and then boldly and purposefully walk up to the stage. Your audience will notice the brilliance that radiates from you at first glance. They will be pleased with and receptive to the confidence your stride and squared shoulders exude. Their enhanced sense of acceptance and happiness will inspire you to perform whole-heartedly. Remember, the road to creative excellence is a two-way street and is filled with support and good vibes between speaker and audience.

Hand Gestures

Have you ever watched Asian dancers from India, Indonesia, Japan, or Thailand? They have these exotic dance routines where the story behind the dance is beautifully and eloquently expressed through the movement of limbs backed up by facial expressions.

You may have also seen people communicate through graceful hand movements and expressions. These dances and sign languages can be mesmerizing to watch because they create such clear images.

Most of us, especially the auditory learners, are not so proficient with using our hands. But hand gestures are very powerful and effective visuals. Imagine the impact of hitting your fist into an open palm when insisting upon a point. Imagine the effect of placing your right hand on your heart while talking about personal things, and imagine the honesty expressed when you spread open both your palms towards your audience. With appropriate gestures, you can increase impact and enhance connectivity with the audience.

Here are some pointers on how to keep your gestures natural, effective and in sync with your words:

- Start with hands loosely held over your belly-button area, prayer style.
- Visualize your head and your body down to your waist level enclosed in an imaginary frame like a photograph. Work your gestures from within that framework. Any gestures that go out of the frame will appear loud and sometimes impolite.
- Do not point your index finger at the audience. No! You are not Uncle Sam that says, "I want you" with a scowl on his face and his index finger pointing! Instead use an open, upward facing palm.

- Let your hand movements be in sync with your words. When you say “big” raise your hands high. When you say “small” lower your hands with palms facing downwards.
- When you want to convey excitement rub your hands together and lean forward.

All through managing your body language, your facial expression and your hand gestures do remember that mind and body are one linked system. What you feel and think in your mind will show through your body and actions and what you do with your body and movements will have an effect on your mind. Therefore, think and practice rhythm and resonance in all public speaking interactions.

Using Mind Mapping® as a Memory Enhancer

Mind Mapping® works in two ways:

First, it is a thought-grabber. It takes quick, colorful and creative notes in visual form of all that occurs in your conscious mind.

Mind Mapping® also works very well in taking long, linear text and converting it to a 2-dimensional, colorful image that becomes a picture and therefore becomes easier to absorb and recall.

We are aware that written text is made up of key ideas expressed in words held together by articles, conjunctions, and prepositions. These three things are easily interchangeable, but what remain essential in any text are the key words: nouns and verbs. Verbs represent the action performed by nouns. If we remember all the nouns and verbs that are keys to a written text, we can then remember the whole speech.

Here are 7 steps to quickly memorize a page of written text:

1. Read through the whole text at an even pace.
2. Every paragraph represents a concept. Note the concepts.
3. Take a black marker and cover all nonessential words like "this, that, where, because, if, for, from, to, etc."
4. Soft-focus on the page again and see if you can still continue reading without the nonessential words.
5. Take the black marker again and cover descriptive words like "big, small, beautiful, enormous, dynamic, etc."
6. Look at the page again and see if you can still continue reading using alternate descriptive words.
7. Continue the exercise until there are very few words left on the page which still express the essence and the message behind every paragraph.

You will notice that the words that are left behind are words that you can relate to and words that help bring back the whole idea behind the text. You will also notice that most of the words left uncovered are nouns and verbs. When you stand up to speak, you will be able to remember and deliver the complete speech using different articles, conjunctions and adjectives, but the essence of the subject matter will remain the same.

This exercise is Mind Mapping® in reverse. It is a memory enhancer. The words that are eventually left behind can be used as key words to create a Mind Map® of the text.

Rehearsing in Reality

At this stage, I believe, you have finished researching, planning, writing, and preparing internally and externally for your speech. Your content, timing, visuals, and handouts are ready. Pending minor revisions and editing, you are now ready to do a final dress rehearsal.

Many folks will tell you that it is best to rehearse in private, preferably in front of the mirror. We often see speakers going into a corner, murmuring to themselves.

Well, you are not doing a high school oral exam. You will be talking to people–lots of them, and the techniques above don't quite work.

To rehearse in reality you've got to create the scenario, in your mind and in reality, as it is actually going to happen. Have a group of friends or your family sit in front of you and listen to you. As you try out your speech on them, stay aware of your pacing, body language, and maintain eye contact. You will see a myriad of expressions flick across their faces. For every word you utter or every expression that you make, there will be a reflection on their faces. If you are going too fast, you will see them lean back. If your material is too deep and jargon-filled, you will see their brows cross and wrinkle. If you are saying simple, pleasant things, you will see them smile.

After you have finished speaking they may respond with polite and affirmative things to you. I recommend you practice reading faces. Then take your own observations and their comments as a set of complete feedback.

Practicing your speech by just reading it out loud to yourself or into a tape or video recorder and in front of a mirror is fine – until a certain point. To connect better with people, you have to try it on real people.

The more times you do a dress rehearsal, the better your delivery and connectivity will become. Do not practice mechanical movements. Practice connectivity and dialogue. Try it out on different people to refrain from boring the same people with the same speech again and again.

Remember to stay flexible with your words and sentences. You may have written beautiful words, but while speaking, it is possible that you forget the exact words. Remember the message that you need to deliver and the objectives that you need to meet.

Here are additional tips on how to practice your speech:

- Read your speech into a tape recorder and play it back while driving, exercising, or relaxing.

- Create a Mind Map® of the key points with images and connections and post it on a wall or a door for frequent reviewing. Your speech will become a picture and will be easier to remember.
- Have someone else read you back your speech. Hearing your own words and thoughts in someone else's voice adds another dimension and leaves a different sensory trace in your mind.

Feedback: Giving and Receiving

I think the first virtue is to restrain the tounge; He approaches nearest to Gods who knows How to be silent, even though he is in the right.

- Cato, the Elder

Many years ago, I was reading a book called True Freedom by a Buddhist Monk from Australia. In one of the anecdotes in the book, the author, a senior monk, relates a story of how one time he was extremely upset at a younger, junior monk who had not followed clear, specific instructions. Because of this, their monastery would suffer serious financial setbacks.

The senior monk had called for the junior monk and was sitting in his room brooding over the losses, his anger, and why the junior monk had not followed instructions. He was also visualizing the would-be interrogation when he realized that he was in a rage and that he was not thinking right.

As he reflected upon his own state of mind, a realization came to him: because he was only focusing on the disobedience and the possible damages, he was not analyzing the issue correctly. He realized that he might not be able to judge fairly and thereby prevent himself and everyone else in the monastery from making the same mistakes again.

He quieted down internally and focused his attention on the junior monk at fault. In his mind, he visualized the youth and his lack of experience. He ran through his mind the behavior and all the past-performances of the junior monk. He realized that the junior monk had always been supportive of his ideas and suggestions. He was selfless, dedicated to the vision of the monastery, and had done a lot of good work over the past years. He became filled with compassion and a deeper wisdom overtook him.

As he concluded his thinking, his thoughts went back to a few moments ago when he was in a rage and wanted to put the junior monk to task for failing. He came to the decision that he would be empathic, objective, and calm. He would focus on the larger issue, solve the current problem, and create a positive and hopeful atmosphere for the future.

Giving and receiving feedback, whether in public speaking skills or on other matters, is just like that. It does not matter whether you are evaluating your own self, your peers or someone junior. Feedback has to be empathic, objective, and motivating.

Feedback must not come from a purely negative point of view, but must take in the big picture. Look at the good points, offer suggestions for improvement, and support positive change. The idea is to make the good in a person grow and develop, to isolate weak areas, and provide specific solutions and the rationale behind them. The person being evaluated needs to understand and accept weaknesses and needs to believe in the values behind the suggestions for improvement.

If you follow this principle while giving feedback to others, then it follows naturally that you will also start treating yourselves with care and objectivity, thereby increasing your self-worth. Such feedback follows the principle of knowing oneself, accepting the environment, and working towards improving all that surrounds you.

Here are steps on how to give feedback to speakers:

- Understand the speaker's objectives well.
- Make an effort to understand what is being meant besides what is being said.
- Provide feedback only on the presentations and not on the speaker's persona.
- Avoid generalization and being judgmental.
- Stay positive, upbeat, and inspire the speaker into being his best.

Fear and Anxiety: All over again.

Remember where fear comes from and how much of that fear comes from your imagination?

- You fear that you may make a fool of yourself.
- You fear that you may not be good enough.
- You fear that others know and understand the subject better than you.

You have done your homework, yet as you approach the time to present, you suffer the jitters and the doubts resurface all over again.

Listed below are external things that you can do which help you alleviate that fear.

- Have a full night's sleep before the event.
- Avoid heavy food and drinks the night before and on the morning of your speaking event.
- Avoid coffee, liquor, tobacco, and medications that reduce alertness.
- Avoid trying to add new lines and phrases to the speech on the eleventh hour. It takes a while for the brain to own additions and new material.
- A few hours before the speaking event, let your mind delve on other matters that are not stressful. This will help settle your nerves and give the speech material time to "settle" and become your own.

Preparation and self-pacification will calm whatever nervousness and anxiety that remains. It will convert your energy to passion and enthusiasm once you lay your eyes on the audience and say to yourself "What I have is mine, it is good, and will be beneficial to my listeners."

Here's a little story about how I once overcame my jitters:

THE NIGHT OF THE JITTERS

I was once invited to compére a dinner function where there were several speakers. The chief amongst them was a lady Philippine presidential candidate. My job was to stay within the theme of the evening, introduce the speakers, and keep the transitions lively, entertaining and contextual.

Easy? Yes, if not for an audience of over a 400 people!

Weeks and days before the event, I gathered the material, read the resumes of the luminaries, prepared my lines and timing. On the day before the event, I had everything down to a pat. But at night in bed, the next day seemed bigger and scarier than most other days.

I tossed and turned restlessly until late into the night. Finally, when I did sleep, I had a nightmare. In the nightmare, I was up on the stage next to all the speakers. The lights were strong on my face. Awed by the crowd, I was in a state of shock. Suddenly, from nowhere the lady chief guest walked up to me, handed me the microphone and said, "Raju, it is your turn! "

My turn! I grappled with the dozen or so pages in my hands and walked up to the lectern. At the lectern, my papers flew from my hand and circled around me in slow motion. The microphone turned into a cobra and stared me down. And, when I looked down at my finely dressed audience they had changed. In their place were people of all kinds. I saw fishermen, street hawkers, and gaunt-faced ladies with cigarettes dangling from their lips. On the floor there were hundreds of crawling babies screaming at their mothers to stop smoking and pay attention to them. My wife was in the crowd begging everyone to calm down and listen to me, the speaker!

The back of the hall had somehow changed into a railway compartment with dozens of big, African-American men playing basketball in it. Big, burly men with beer mugs in their hands were watching the game while the train of my speaking moment was hurtling away towards nowhere!

In the nightmare, I heard someone knock at the door of the railway compartment. Covered in cold sweat, I woke up with a scream in my throat! As I sat up in bed, I recognized the absurdity of the whole situation. The demons of anxiety and fear were playing games with my mind.

The knocking on my bedroom door was real, and I walked up to it and opened it. There stood my little 7-year-old daughter, crying for her mother. I picked her up and held her against me. My fears subsided and a smile took over my jitters and doubts.

I was overcome by an inner peace and calm. I went to sleep assured that tomorrow, I was going to perform for a crowd not go to war with the world. My fears were gone and the material that I had been working upon became mine. The next day I dazzled the crowd and the lady chief guest at the dinner function.

Sometimes, all the external preparations and research will not help much until the conviction comes from inside and you are able to reclaim your strength and confidence from within.

5.0 Insights on Practicing a Speech

5.1 When you are anxious, your psyche literally strangles your breathing. Breathe consciously and deliberately to get rid of anxiety. Once you are free of anxiety, your systems will work in resonance.

5.2 Your physical appearance, posture and gestures are a language by themselves. Be conscious of them and use them well for higher impact.

5.3 Practice speaking clearly and often. Recognize and maintain your most pleasing and impressive voice.

5.4 Pause between words; it's like breathing between gasps. You and your audience need it.

5.5 Memorize the essential points of your speech and then keep the speech conversational yet focused.

5.6 Practice your speeches on people and not just with mirrors, tape recorders, or the wall. You need to get feedback.

5.7 Practice and prepare meticulously. This will help you gain confidence.

5.0 Exercises

Read the following sentences and note the change in meaning by stressing the underlined words.

I was born in Singapore!
[I and not someone else was born in Singapore.]

I ***was*** born in Singapore!
[I am very sure it was Singapore and not any other place.]

I was ***born*** in Singapore!
[I was born in Singapore and I should know!]

I was born ***in*** Singapore!
[I was born within the limits of Singapore, not outside it.]

I was born in ***Singapore!***
[I am so glad it was Singapore and I am proud of it.]

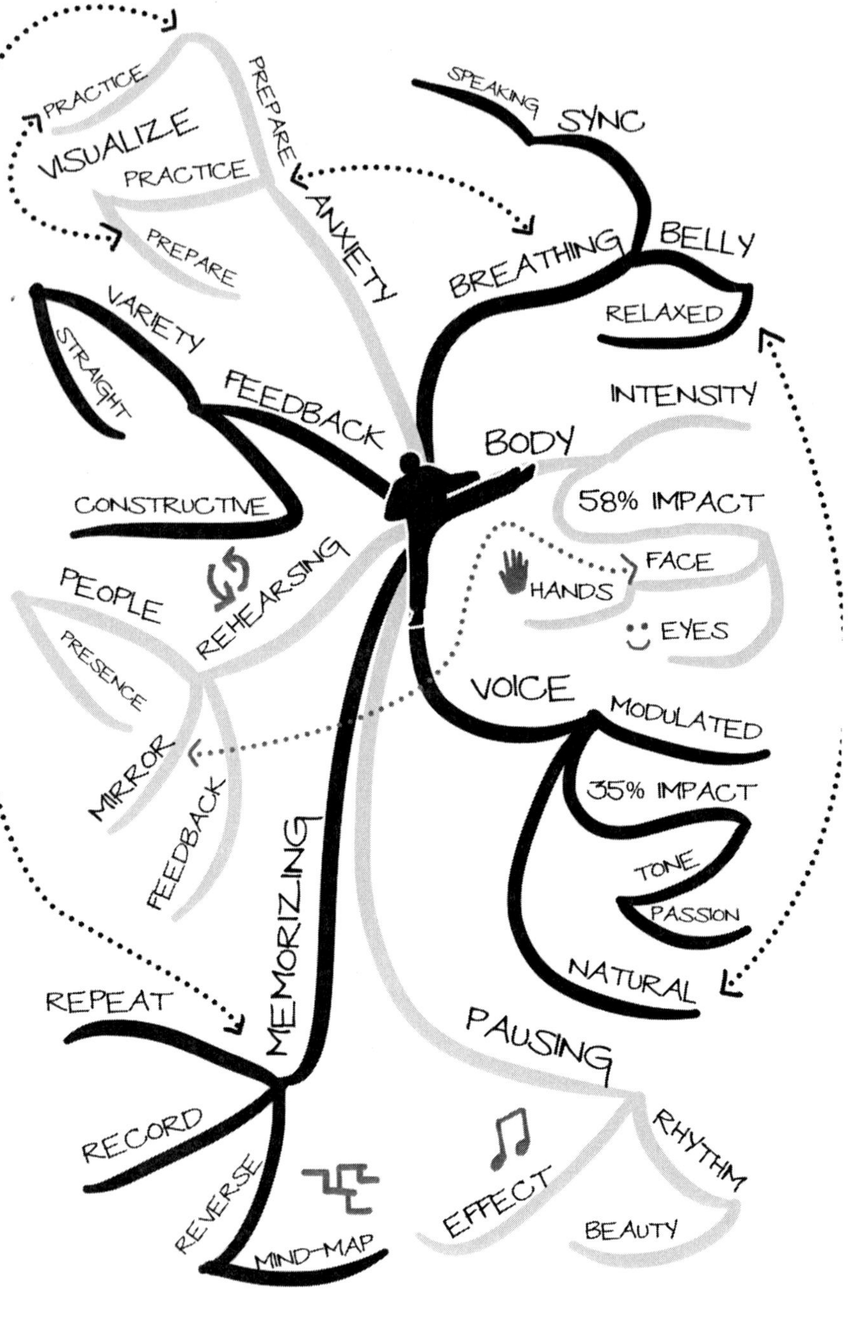
PRACTICE
VISUALIZE
PRACTICE
PREPARE
PREPARE
ANXIETY
SPEAKING
SYNC
BREATHING
BELLY
RELAXED
VARIETY
STRAIGHT
FEEDBACK
CONSTRUCTIVE
INTENSITY
BODY
58% IMPACT
FACE
HANDS
EYES
PEOPLE
PRESENCE
REHEARSING
MIRROR
FEEDBACK
VOICE
MODULATED
35% IMPACT
TONE
PASSION
NATURAL
MEMORIZING
REPEAT
RECORD
REVERSE
MIND-MAP
PAUSING
RHYTHM
EFFECT
BEAUTY

Chapter Six
How to Deliver a Speech

There are people who, instead of listening to what is being said to the them, are already listening to what they are going to say themselves.

- Albert Guirron

The John McEnroe Technique

Professional tennis players who spend a lifetime preparing and practicing for championship games are also exposed to the kinds of jitters we experience as public speakers.

Tennis players are exposed to thousands of cheering and jeering audiences, television cameras, and glaring spotlights. Through this, they need to stay positive, visualize success, and give their very best every time they step up to the net. Many tennis players are known to have breakdowns from all the pressure.

To overcome his anxiety and fear of public scrutiny, John McEnroe follows a certain technique that I believe works very well for public speakers too. On the morning of a game, before all the spectators and the cameras arrive, he goes to the court and drops down on all fours, makes faces, lies on his back, and does all the foolish things that he fears he might do while in the middle of a game. He screams, cries, makes faces, and dances like crazy. The process exorcises all his fears and jitters of public exposure to come later.

When he does eventually return to the court, the memory of his "stupid" behavior in the morning strengthens him against any "stupidity" that he might commit on court. His personal resolve after his antics strengthens, and he plays coolly and calmly.

I have known speakers who get up on stage before the event, test the sound system, try out their vocal chords, and say a few lines from the speech. In that way, they overcome performance anxiety and any inhibitions that may arise during delivery of the speech.

Revisiting Self, Audience, and the Message

Stories of Muhammad Ali mention how before his prizefights, he would enter the ring and go down on his knees for a few moments. In those few moments, all his hopes, visions, and fears would flash past him. In that meditative moment, Muhammad Ali would revisit all his physical and mental training. One by one, he would tick off his worries and focus on exactly what he wanted to do in the next few rounds.

The fear of public speaking is considered worse than the fear of death, but I bet that it is not as scary as being in a boxing ring for 20 minutes with a menacing heavyweight challenger!

If prizefighters review their training and plans before each fight, we public speakers should likewise revisit our plans. A few minutes before you get to the lectern, do a self-evaluation, bring your attention back to audience needs, and refocus on the message.

Doing this exercise is the equivalent of saying a prayer. It is a serene, meditative moment where you can overcome the last of your anxieties and enter the ring of public speaking with faith and confidence. This meditative moment can be in the form of questions directed at your inner being.

Before your presentation, meditate on the following:

- Is this public speaking event about making me look good?
- Is this public speaking just about promoting my product or proposal?
- Or is it about doing something good and valuable for all the people who have come to hear me?

The answers you receive from your inner being are truths. As long as your answers are honest and non-critical, you will end up speaking with power and authenticity.

Listening Mindfully

The other day at the bank, Lisa, my young and attractive bank officer was telling me how her mother had taken a fall, and while waiting for hip replacement, was confined in a hospital in the USA.

While Lisa was talking to me, I was watching her eyebrows and wondering how painful it must be for girls to undergo all that plucking. I was wondering how she would look if she let her eyebrows grow. As soon as she was done speaking I looked up and brightly asked her, "Hey, how's your mom? Does she still live in Japan?" Right! I was hearing her but I hadn't been listening! Listening requires engagement, comprehension, absorption, and processing while hearing is only a function of the ears.

We spend half of our waking time communicating with others and the other half listening. In school we are taught how to read, write, and recite, but have any of us spent time learning to listen fully? If we learned to listen with our heads and hearts, we'd be able to manage our time projects, and plans much more efficiently.

Putting our heads and hearts together makes us not just attentive, but also watchful of our own input. At our workshops from Inner Sun Consultants, we call this becoming MindFul.

Listening Mindfully will benefit you by:

- Making you aware of your own intentions and authenticity.
- Strengthening and improving your relationships with your colleagues and community.
- Giving you the ability to bring about positive and meaningful change in the world.

Listening Mindfully can be achieved by taking these five simple steps:

1. **Investigate** Intentions. Before entering any conversation, find out what it is that you really want to achieve. An honest appraisal of your intentions will keep you open and interested in new ideas. The brainstorming ability of Mind Mapping® will help you understand your own needs.

2. **Increase** Awareness. While you are listening, clear your mental clutter. This could be anything from nagging thoughts, to lists of things to do, to plans for the day. Postpone these thoughts, increase awareness, note change in tone, and pitch and pace of speaker. Look for underlying feelings and visualize your mind storing information in key words and images just as in Mind Mapping®.

3. **Interact** with Interest and Enthusiasm. Listening is not done just with your ears. It is also done with your eyes and body. Maintain eye contact and lean towards the speaker. Every now and then blink with approval, nod, and smile or participate gently by uttering words like "uh-uh," "hmmm," "gee!" or "wow!" Keep this participation genuine and gentle.

4. **Inquire** and Re-Phrase. All transfer of information, knowledge, or ideas from one mind to another generally leaves a small percentage of the unknown. Clarify and fill that gap as much as possible by making simple, direct, and inoffensive questions. Rephrase ideas or create comparisons to further solidify understanding.

5. **Imprint** Impressions. This is possible in meetings or conferences where more than three people are involved and they may take turns at communicating. The quick, colorful, note-taking feature of Mind Mapping® will help you put down your impressions and review ideas and perceptions later.

Following these five simple steps will help you enhance your listening skills. Improved listening skills will help you absorb more, clarify more, and be able to make better creative and conscientious decisions about people, issues, and perceptions.

And, the next time you are in a bank with an attractive bank officer, it would help to keep your mind on your listening. History repeats itself only because people do not listen mindfully the first time!

Becoming the Heart and Soul of the Crowd

In Chapter 4, Section 3 we discussed the three entities in a public speaking event - you, "the little person on your shoulder," and the audience. Until now, you have done a lot of work regarding fear or faith from that "little person."

Everything that you have planned, prepared, and practiced will be put to test. If you have done all the "inner" and the "outer" work, by now you are with the audience and for the audience.

Every word you utter is smooth, specific, and entertaining. Your audience's mood, their state of mind and their vision are now in sync with your mood, state of mind, and vision.

This is when you must let go of yourself. Roll with the punches. You are feeling free, in control, and powerful. Realize that the power is coming not only from you, but also from the resonance provided by the presence of the sheer number of people in your audience.

These are the highlights of any public speaking event. The moment you respond with agility, flow with abandon, and drop all pretensions and fears, you have become the heart and soul of a speaking moment. This is the time to take yourself to the next level of excellence as a speaker and person.

Staying Sensitive, Connected, and Thriving on the Momentum

While you are on a roll with your speech and the audience is in the palm of your hand, take caution and remember that these moments of exhilaration are moments where speakers tend to feel overconfident and tumble into disastrous slips.
Even as you achieve your speaking high, remember common courtesy, authenticity, and the fact that as the speaker you create change. Therefore, focus on bringing about positive change.

Stay sensitive to audience feelings and reactions. Watch their body language. Read their eyes and other non-verbal forms of communication. Watch out for people fidgeting or leaning back stiffly or knitting their brows from lack of understanding. In your excited state, learn to pause, stop, reflect and respond. If you know your material well and have faith in you message, a pause will not derail your presentation.

Stay connected through interjections, questions, and dialogue, but stay focused on your message. Persuading a group of people to a proposition is like shepherding a bunch of sheep into a yard. You have to be gentle yet quick. You have to keep your eyes on the herd and not allow a single lamb to stray.

When you and your audience are both enjoying the talk, it is time to build and grow on the momentum. Finish all that you have to say, add more if you wish. Ask and answer questions that will clear any gaps and bridge understanding.

Here are other tips on how to thrive on the momentum:

- React emotionally to the audience rather than just intellectually.
- Thrive on the adrenaline and the nervous rush.
- Work from the gut and follow your intuition.
- As you merge with your audience, you will realize that you have become the message.

Raju Mandhyan

Facing Open Forums with Finesse

Treat the other man's faith gently;
it is all he has to believe with.
His mind was created for his own
thoughts, Not yours or mine.

- Henry S. Haskins

The question and answer part after most presentations serves to gauge what the presentation may not have achieved.

A public speaking activity is really a transfer of information, ideas, or inspiration from one mind (the speaker's) to several minds (the audience's)... Even though a speaker may have done all the research, planning, and preparation, there will always be a certain amount of gap, doubts, and clarifications after the delivery. Absorption and integration of knowledge take time for acceptance and eventual incubation.

A good question and answer section at the end of every presentation will reduce information gaps, eliminate doubts, and enhance clarity.

- Questions must be given sincere attention and respect.
- Questions must be judged from the perspective of the one asking the question rather than from the one who answers them.
- The answers to all questions must be precise, polite, and sufficient.
- If you do not have the answers or are in doubt of the facts, say so and seek permission to get back to the query.
- Questions from the floor must be taken from random people and the replies must be given to the inquirer and the audience.

In high school Physics, we were taught the concept of an Absolute Black Body which is high on absorption of energy radiated at it. In reality, there is no element known to man that can absorb a hundred percent of all energy radiated at it but an Absolute Black Body, which is a theoretical construct, tends to absorb 99.99% of all light energy radiated at it.

In the same sense knowledge and wisdom, which are energy forms, can never be transferred a hundred percent from one person to another. A good lot is lost in the medium of conversation, in interpretation and in the latent resistance of every listener. To overcome this and to maximize transfer, it is important that gaps in understanding be filled through questions and answers after every presentation. All open forums, thus, are important as they reduce doubts and enhance clarity and acceptance of all ideas and proposals.

6.0 Insights on Delivering a Speech

6.1 The fear of looking awkward or silly can be overcome by practicing where you have to perform.

6.2 An internal dialogue about your objectives works like a prayer before the performance.

6.3 Listening well is necessary to thinking well, and thinking well leads to communicating well.

6.4 Learn to draw energy y from the audience participation.

6.5 Mind your language. Stay politically correct and conscious of the audience's cultural sensitivities.

6.6 The question and answer period is necessary to fill gaps in information transfer.

6.7 Your mood and attitude will influence the mood and attitude of your audience.

6.0 Exercises

1. List down at least three things you can do to become calm and controlled.

2. While speaking, list at least 3 non-verbal reactions of the audience that you need to keep an eye on. (For example: They are leaning forward attentively).

3. List at least three things about content and delivery that you need to be careful about while speaking.

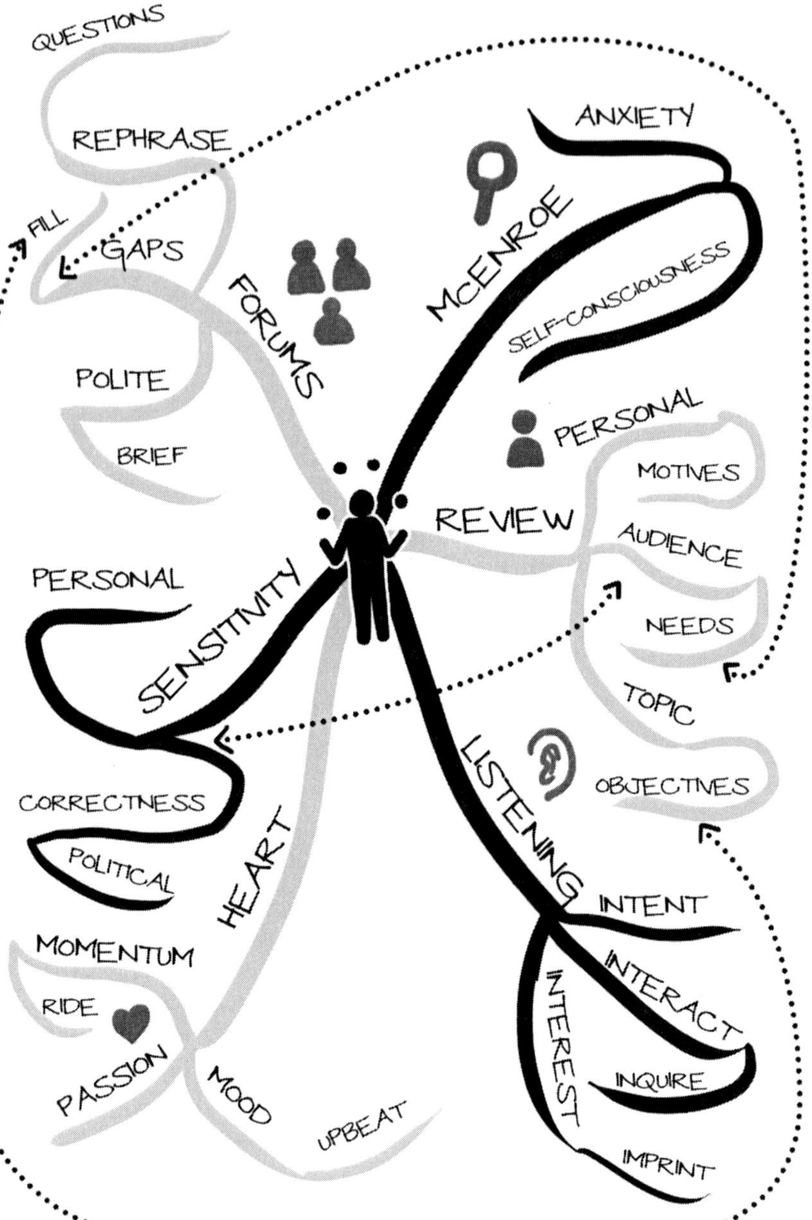
QUESTIONS
REPHRASE
FILL
GAPS
FORUMS
POLITE
BRIEF
ANXIETY
McENROE
SELF-CONSCIOUSNESS
PERSONAL
MOTIVES
REVIEW
AUDIENCE
NEEDS
TOPIC
OBJECTIVES
PERSONAL
SENSITIVITY
CORRECTNESS
POLITICAL
HEART
MOMENTUM
RIDE
PASSION
MOOD
UPBEAT
LISTENING
INTENT
INTERACT
INTEREST
INQUIRE
IMPRINT

Chapter Seven
Continuously Improving as a Speaker and a Human Being

Success isn't a result of spontaneous combustion.
You must set yourself on fire.

- Arnold Glascow

THE MILLIONAIRE INSIDE

Farmer Juan de la Cruz from Pangasinan, Philippines owned 100 acres of family land. As far as he could remember, neither his father nor his uncles could grow anything on the land. The land was barren, dry and reaped nothing.

Friends told him to dig for oil in the land since the soil formation had dark streaks to it. Juan, with the help of local drillers, dug. He dug in several spots and all the corners of the land but all the digging showed no signs of oil anywhere. Frustrated, Juan signed up some foreign partners and agreed to share 80% if they hit oil.

The new partners went to the center of the arid land, strung up a massive rig and dug. They dug 100 times deeper than Juan and his crew had ever done.

Very soon, they hit oil!
Normally when oil is hit it gushes out and shoots out over the rig. When they hit oil in Juan's land not only did the oil shoot up from the ground, it also ripped out the heavy steel rig from the earth and blew it up far into the sky. They hit oil! Millions of barrels a day!

Oil, those days, was priced at about $20 a barrel. The question arises - did Juan become a millionaire?

On that day when they struck millions of barrels of oil in Juan dela Cruz's land, did farmer Juan de la Cruz become a Millionaire?

The answer is no!

No, Juan de la Cruz did not become a millionaire on the day they found oil on his land. The oil had been laying right under his feet all his life. Juan de la Cruz had always been a millionaire, only he had never dug deep enough into his own property.

All that we need to learn to become good speakers and good human beings lies inside of us. All we need to do is go to the center, dig as we have never dug and find that talisman which will take us higher.

Mastering your Materials and Refining the Message

Whatever your field of expertise or interest, if you want to become good at speaking about it, you must learn as much as possible and constantly increase your knowledge and expertise in your field.

Not only must you dig deeper and study harder, you must also learn fields that are parallel to it. You must also learn and master new ideas and inventions related to your subject matter.

We all have opinions and reasons as to why we stay in a certain field of work: Doctors want to save lives, engineers want to build, and artists want to create.

In each field there is something of value which keeps you there. That value becomes your point of conviction. Once you recognize this value and how it can bring about personal and social good, then you have recognized a message to spread.

Believe deeply in the message that you want to spread, and you will keep on improving as a speaker and as a human being.

Developing Depth and Breadth as a Person

There is an old saying: "Travel broadens a person's mind." I'd like to add, "And surviving sorrow deepens it."

Travel allows you to see the world and experience cultures. Observing the world and its people gives you different perspectives on yourself.

Travel here is also a metaphor for living life vicariously through books, movies, music, arts, and religions. If you want to broaden your perspectives, stretch and expose your mental and spiritual limits.

When I talk about surviving sorrow to achieve depth, I do not mean that one should go seeking sorrow in life so he can survive it. Sorrow and pain are the checks in our lives that keep us balanced. I am talking about reflection and deep introspection that usually accompany sorrow and life in general. Whenever you go through a low period in life, your heart works over time. This also is a time to let your head keep track of what goes on in your heart.

Keeping track of what goes on in your heart during times of pain gives you a better understanding of yourself as a person. It gives you a multitude of insights into the nature of humankind. Observing, acknowledging, and remembering the changes of perspectives that you go through during such times deepen you as a person and as a speaker.

A speaker with depth and breadth is a joy to listen to because his every word is filled with passion, understanding, and truths about the nature of man. Listening to such a speaker becomes soothing and therapeutic.

A speaker that speaks from the heart and structures his talks with his head becomes an authentic speaker.

Learning to Learn Exponentially

"To myself I seemed like a boy playing on the seashore, diverting himself and then finding a smoother pebble or a prettier shell than ordinary, while the great Ocean of truth lay all undiscovered before me."

- Isaac Newton

A growing child picks up words and ideas at a phenomenal rate. This learning accumulates until the child reaches adulthood. Upon adulthood, there is a steady decline of absorption of new words, ideas, and knowledge. In my opinion, one of the main reasons for that is that a person feels that he has acquired all the technical knowledge he needs to move around, feed, and survive. There is, of course, a large percentage of people that break this rule and keep on learning, exploring and experimenting.

These are people who seek awareness and insights beyond what's necessary to survive everyday living. They make a habit out of broadening their perspectives and deepening their understanding of humankind. They read a lot more than most other people. They write more and record their observations, insights, and discoveries. They seek constant feedback about themselves and their progress.

When I was introduced to Mind Mapping® back in 1997, I found a tool that has helped me read and analyze more. It has also helped me express myself more effectively.

The road to learning exponentially is a physical journey. It requires hours of reading, analyzing, and reflecting upon knowledge gained and expressing it in written or spoken form.

Follow these simple steps to transform yourself into a lifelong learner:

- Do not refuse any opportunity to listen to experts.
- Read as much as you can about a wide range of subjects.
- Do not refuse or turn down any opportunity to stand up and speak, however humble the occasion.
- Ask questions constantly about new subjects and re-validate your knowledge.
- Constantly put yourself and your abilities to test. Do not be embarrassed by failure.
- Constantly seek feedback on your speaking style and subject matter expertise.

STORY OF A CEO

Her palms were sweaty and her throat was dry. She clenched her notes and transparencies with shaky hands. As she reached the microphone, she was afraid that the audience would hear her heart – it was thudding wildly in her chest.

As she glanced at the expectant faces of her colleagues she suddenly realized that they knew the truth: She was scared to death. She wasn't sure of what she was going to say and her position at IBM

Philippines was now teetering on a cliff. She had to prove that she was an able and confident young woman.

She felt like crying. She would have given her life and soul to be anywhere else but behind the lectern. Somehow, she was able to mumble her way out of the situation. Later that night, when she was alone, she swore to herself that she would never let something like that happen to her again.

That was nearly twenty-five years ago. Today, Carol Carreon is known as a CEO par excellence. She sits on the board of several multi-national corporations and does a lot of social and civil work. She is constantly on the invitation list of major businesses and social functions organized in the Philippines. In her field of Information Technology, she is referred to as the "Guru."

After that first disastrous event as a young IBM executive, she took it upon herself to master the art and science of public speaking. Something inside her told her that all her past accomplishments as an honor student in school would not amount to anything if she did not learn to express herself with clarity, creativity, and wit. She took up public speaking like one would pursue a doctoral course. Now in her fifties, she constantly speaks, trains, and practices just as doggedly as she did in her twenties. Over the years her public speaking abilities have become the driving force in her life. Today, she listens effectively, thinks with clarity and precision, and speaks with wit and wisdom.

I asked her once, "Carol, as far as public speaking abilities go, do you think you have arrived?" With a twinkle in her eyes she gently answered, "Like Newton, I feel like I am on the edge of an ocean, constantly collecting pebbles while all that is yet to be discovered lies ahead of me."

Varied Exposure to Continuous Evaluation

Twenty years from now you will be more disappointed by the things you didn't do than by the ones you did.
So throw off the bowlines.
Catch the trade winds in your sails.
Explore! Dream! Discover!

- Eleanor Roosevelt

Several years ago, I was attending one of my first Toastmasters' meetings when the president of the club, Advanced Toastmaster Sylvia Mijares, asked me if I could evaluate one of the advanced speakers. I was surprised, "Me? Give feedback to an advanced speaker?"

She responded that feedback was just a summation of your observations, feelings, and thoughts. "Don't worry," she said, "even if you don't know anything about public speaking, the advanced speaker will know what to do with your observations."

There's an old Indian saying that says, "Sometimes from the observations of the ignorant you can hear words of wisdom." So, when it comes to getting constant feedback on your public speaking, go ahead and expose yourself to people from all walks of life and listen to them well. Though they may be ignorant or harsh, pick up points which you know you can use for self-improvement.

Master all the steps as discussed in this book. Maintain an open and positive state of mind and understand where your evaluation comes from. Seek a multitude of speaking opportunities and very soon you will be on your way to becoming an excellent public speaker.

Staying Lofty and Keeping the Faith

Since the dawn of civilization, people have wondered about their source of creation, the purpose of life, and the meaning behind everything we do.

Holy men, philosophers, and thinkers have provided us with several answers, yet the modern man still wonders and doubts his own capabilities.

But turn around and take a look at what mankind has done over the ages. We have mastered fire, built cities and highways, eradicated hundreds of diseases, created symphonies, and flown to the moon and back. We have done many things that would have amazed and stupefied every generation that existed before us.

So, perhaps if we do not have answers to the bigger questions of life, we can acknowledge our progress and make that an answer. Let us keep our faith in the daily chores that we perform and leave the higher questions to be answered, in time, by humanity.

There is a story about the most favored angel who went to the Creator and asked the Creator if he had any favorite beings other than him. He was surprised when the Creator pointed to an ordinary peanut farmer named John Doe in Georgia, USA as His most favorite being.

Envious and angry, the angel flew from the Heavens to Earth and went to observe the lifestyle of John Doe, the peanut farmer. John Doe's daily routine was to wake up, wash up, eat breakfast, bid adieu to his family and go to the farm for work. But as he would step out of the house, John Doe would look up into the skies and whisper a humble "Thank you."

He would toil all day in the farm. Come evening he'd have a drink, shoot some pool, and stumble home to his family. He would love and hug them and soon knock off to sleep. But every time he entered his doorstep, John Doe would look up into the skies and again whisper a humble "Thank you."

The angel was pretty upset at seeing all this and he took the next flight out of Earth to Heaven.

Back in the presence of the Creator, he loudly and angrily explained the boring, humdrum, sinful lifestyle of John Doe and wondered why he was the Creator's favorite being.

The Creator explained with a gentle smile. He said, "John Doe is my favorite being because he does exactly what he is supposed to do as a farmer. And to top it all, he expresses his gratefulness for his living and life twice a day to me. You, on the other hand, have good, angelic work to do, but instead you become insecure about your position, compare notes and become bitter about things."

The lesson is that it doesn't really matter what it is that we do in life but it is how we do it. The lesson is that destinations and achievements are not the ultimate goals. The journey and processes are important too. Whatever it is that we do, we must keep our faith, enjoy life, and thrive on our contribution to humankind and nature.

All it takes is for us to put our heads, hearts, and humor into what we do, and the whole universe will turn around on its axis to provide us with our destinations, achievements, and accolades in life.

Live well, love much, and laugh often. All you need to do to become an excellent public speaker and person is to use your head rationally, put your heart into all you do, and take all your shortcomings lightly.

7.0 Insights on Continuously Improving as a Speaker and a Human Being

7.1 Increasing your knowledge in the subject matter and learning the techniques of delivery will help you improve constantly.

7.2 Learning about parallel and related subject matters will add depth and variety to your dialogue.

7.3 Getting a variety of feedback on your subject and style will help you improve your materials and yourself.

7.4 The more you chase your passion in your work and living, the better a communicator you will become.

7.5 Go beyond your limits, stay selfless, and include community in your work.

7.0 Exercises

1. Why is the underlying message in most public talks important?

____

____

____

____

____

2. List down at least three things you can do to become an excellent communicator and person.

____

____

____

____

____

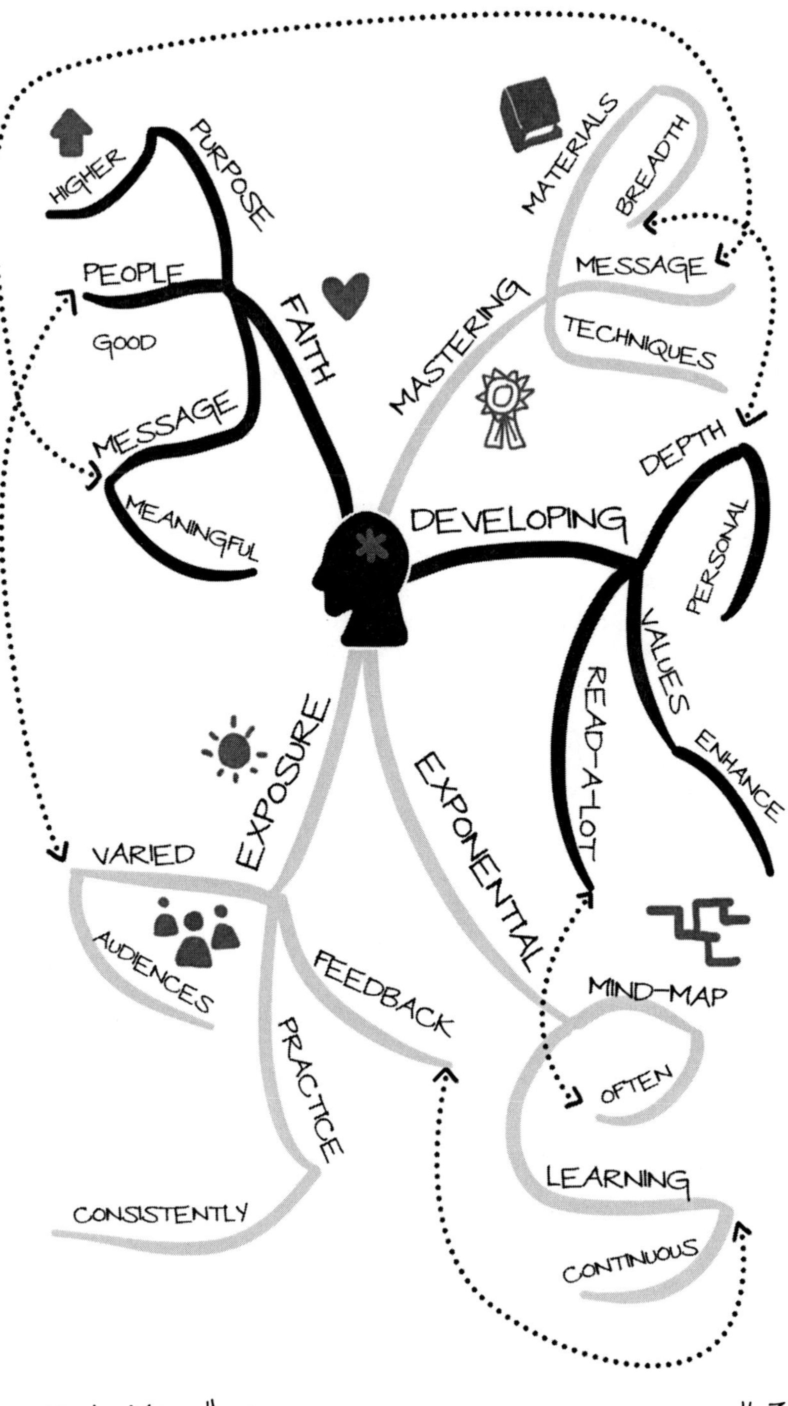
HIGHER
PURPOSE
PEOPLE
GOOD
MESSAGE
MEANINGFUL
FAITH
MATERIALS
BREADTH
MESSAGE
TECHNIQUES
MASTERING
DEPTH
DEVELOPING
PERSONAL
VALUES
ENHANCE
READ-A-LOT
EXPOSURE
EXPONENTIAL
VARIED
AUDIENCES
FEEDBACK
PRACTICE
CONSISTENTLY
MIND-MAP
OFTEN
LEARNING
CONTINUOUS

Mind Maps®...

A Mind Map® on How to Mind Map®
A Mind Map® of Researching for a Speech
A Mind Map® of Planning for a Speech
A Mind Map® of Writing for a Speech
A Mind Map® of Preparing for a Speech
A Mind Map® of Practicing a Speech
A Mind Map® of Delivering a Speech
A Mind Map® of Continuously Improving as a Speaker and a Human Being,

Exercises...

1.0 Researching for a Speech
2.0 Planning for a Speech
3.0 Writing a Speech
4.0 Preparing for Speaking
5.0 Practicing a Speech
6.0 Delivering a Speech
7.0 Continuously Improving as a Speaker & a Human Being

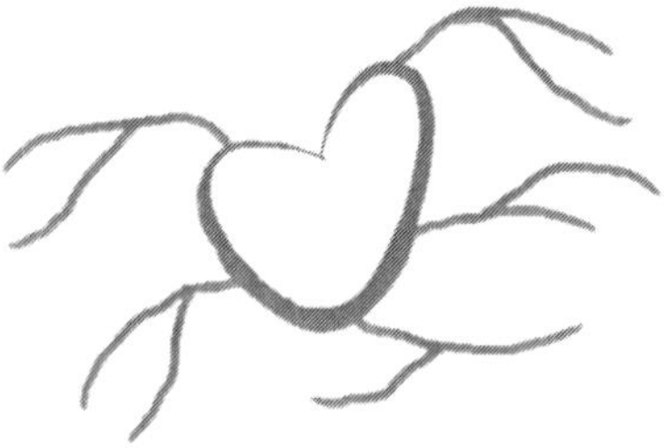

About Inner Sun...

We at Inner Sun believe that every individual and every organization is a living system. At any given moment in this living system, there are three dimensions continuously at play.

The first is the dynamism that is innate, congenital, and embedded. In an individual, it is sometimes referred to as nature or personality; in a business organization, it may be referred to as "work culture".

The second dynamism is the one that exists outside of this system and is of many forms; the way that it is often referred to is the environment, economy, or ecology.

The third, the most vibrant, with a high potential to influence the inner and the outer dynamisms, is the dynamics of the process between the internal and external systems. The drivers of this intermediate dynamism are awareness, intelligence, emotion, memory, and action.

Inner Sun, the organization, focuses its own awareness, intelligence, and action towards this intermediary dynamism in all endeavors and interventions. The guiding elements behind our endeavors and interventions are:

Clarity of thought, words, and action;
Creativity of design, approach, and strategy; and,
Conscientiousness of purpose and ultimate objectives.

Thinking free of bias and mental hammerlocks leads to higher clarity, creativity, and conscientiousness. As individuals and organizations strive for that status, their intelligences expand, interests broaden, and achievements soar.

We provide:

- Business solutions and interventions that bring about measurable results;
- Trainers who judge success not on their own performances but by how much the delegates learn;
- Personal service and tons of great value in an atmosphere of inspiration, support, and motivation;

For details and a list of updated programs, please log on to www.mandhyan.com

About Raju Mandhyan

Author of five books, Cross-Cultural Leadership Coach and Learning Facilitator Raju Mandhyan has 15 years of experience in personal and organizational development. He has coached thousands of executives, delivered keynotes for hundreds of conferences across the Asian-Pacific region.

He is certified in Neuro Linguistic Programming, Mind Mapping, Appreciative Inquiry, American Management Association's Train the Trainer. He is also a Distinguished Toastmaster, Champion Speaker and the 2005-District Champion for Evaluations in the Philippines. In 2010, he had the rare honor of presenting at the American Society of Training and Development annual conference in Chicago.

Prior to his consulting career, Raju spent two years as an Engineer, two years as a Financial Consultant and 17 years as the CEO of an International Mercantile company handling projects for clients across the Mediterranean, Europe, Latin and North Americas. He has lived in India, USA and now lives with wife and three kids in the Philippines.

Look him up at www.mandhyan.com

other works

THE HEART OF HUMOR

TALES AND TECHNIQUES FOR A CREATIVELY FUNNIER YOU AT HOME AND AT WORK

Powerful and profound insights into what exactly humor is and backed by tales and techniques which, after practice, will make you a better observer of things, an acute and sensitive listener, a clearer and a faster thinker; an entertaining host and speaker and finally an all-around happy and wholesome person to be with.

THE HEART OF STORY

CONNECT, ENGAGE AND INFLUENCE YOUR AUDIENCE CREATIVELY.

This is a fantastic job of bringing to our consciousness the what, why, and how of corporate storytelling. Stories are realities wrapped in roses, rainbows, and rhythm. This is, after all, what a company needs to sell, to build its brand, to communicate with stakeholders, and to drive creativity and innovation. THE HEART OF STORY is beautifully written and is such a smooth read.

THE HEART OF THE CLOSE

SUBTLE CLOSING STRATEGIES TO SOAR BEYOND YOUR SALES TARGETS

This book underscores a natural appreciation for the sales process. More than the "how-to's," real-life experience and wit weave throughout the book and how simplifies complex concepts. This amazingly insightful book comes at an opportune time, when the intricacies of selling in this milieu invite a more evolved appreciation for being human than a successful sales person

.

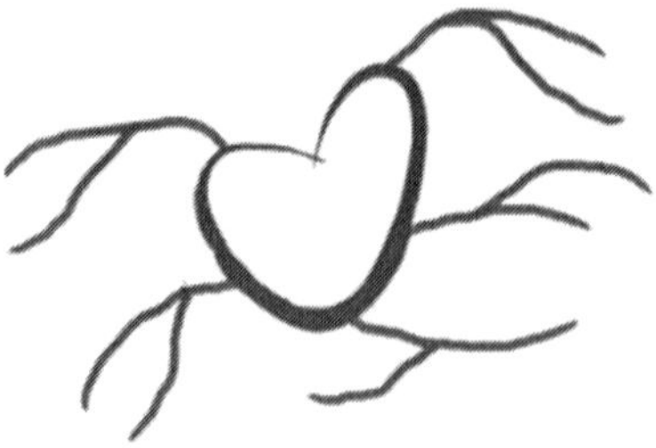

As your dreams are, so shall be your deeds.
As your deeds are, so shall be your destiny.